Anonymus

Theosophy Exposed - Mrs. Besant and her Guru

Anonymus

Theosophy Exposed - Mrs. Besant and her Guru

ISBN/EAN: 9783742867087

Manufactured in Europe, USA, Canada, Australia, Japa

Cover: Foto ©Lupo / pixelio.de

Manufactured and distributed by brebook publishing software (www.brebook.com)

Anonymus

Theosophy Exposed - Mrs. Besant and her Guru

THEOSOPHY EXPOSED.

OR,

Mrs. BESANT AND HER GURU.

AN

APPEAL TO EDUCATED HINDUS.

PRINCIPAL CONTENTS.

The exposure of Madame Blavatsky by the Madras Christian College Magazine; the Report of the Psychical Research Society; Critical Historical Review of the Theosophical Society; Proofs of the ignorance and trickery of Madame Blavatsky; with an account of Mrs. Besant and her many changes of belief, showing her to be a most unsafe religious guide.

MADRAS:
THE CHRISTIAN LITERATURE SOCIETY.
S. P. C. K. PRESS, VEPERY.

1893.

THE VISIT OF MRS. BESANT.

AN APPEAL TO INDIAN JOURNALISTS

AND

INTELLIGENT HINDUS.

About fifteen years ago, MADAME BLAVATSKY, accompanied by COLONEL OLCOTT, landed in India to make converts to Theosophy, defined as the WISDOM RELIGION. She claimed to have studied for years under Mahatmas in Tibet, and to have acquired from them wonder-working powers which she exhibited from time to time.

During her absence in Europe, two of her confederates were expelled from the "Brotherhood," and, as often happens in such cases, the truth came out. Seventy or eighty of Madame Blavatsky's own letters, with other evidence, proved that she was an impostor. She asserted that they were, in whole or in part, forgeries; but when challenged publicly to prove it in a court of justice, she prudently declined.

Madame Blavatsky commenced a journal called *The Theosophist*. It was thus noticed by *The Saturday Review*:—

"*The Theosophist* is full of translations from the works of ancient 'theurgists,' of 'spirit communications,' and of blatant nonsense of all kinds, flavoured with the pseudo-science and second-hand archæology which distinguish 'trance lectures' and the utterances of 'materialized spirits.' Our old friend Zadkiel, too, has a good word said for him. '*Omne ignotum pro magnifico*' is a trite adage; and we dare say that all this rubbish presents itself to the Hindu mind as serious Western lore.

"A clumsy attempt has been made to spread the false and pernicious doctrines of 'Spiritualism' among the too impressionable inhabitants of India, and to bolster up the balderdash with pseudo-oriental learning which will not bear for one moment the test of scholarly criticism."[*]

---

[*] Quoted in *Bombay Gazette*, Sept. 28, 1881.

THE VISIT OF MRS. BESANT.

Professor Max Müller, in the last May issue of *The Nineteenth Century*, corroborates the above opinion. In *Isis Unveiled*, written professedly by Madame Blavatsky and the Mahatmas, some of "the most ordinary terms are misspelt and misunderstood."

The Society for Psychical Research sent out Mr. R. Hodgson, a Cambridge graduate, to examine carefully the evidence in support of the alleged "phenomena." His lengthy Account was summed up in a Report of the Committee, written by Professor Sidgwick. The "phenomena" were characterised as fraudulent, and the proof was considered "irresistible" that the Mahatma Koot Hoomi, *i. e.*, Madame Blavatsky, was a plagiarist and liar.

Nine years after the above exposure, Mrs. Besant comes to India, professing to believe in the "phenomena" and to have seen a Mahatma. Womanlike, moved apparently by "*the proud fiery truthfulness that shown at her from the clear blue eyes of Madame Blavatsky,—honest and fearless as those of a noble child,*" she "flung aside" Professor Sidgwick's Report " with righteous scorn."

Her profession of Hinduism, her outrageous flattery of everything Indian, and her vilification of England, have made her immensely popular among ignorant and half-educated Hindus. In a telegram from Bangalore she is styled "the veritable goddess of Ind, coming from the far off West for the spiritual regeneration of the land."

Apart from Mrs. Besant's religious views, her influence is very injurious. She is reported to speak of "Western learning and Western civilization with undisguised contempt." She sides with the "Orientalists," who were so signally defeated during Lord William Bentinck's administration. Macaulay says in his celebrated "Minute":—

"What we spend on the Arabic and Sanskrit Colleges is not merely a dead loss to the cause of truth; it is bounty-money paid to raise up champions of error. It goes to form a nest, not merely of helpless place hunters, but of bigots prompted alike by passion and interest to raise a cry against every useful scheme of education."

Thirty years later, Sir H. S. Maine, a distinguished successor of Macaulay as Law Member, expressed similar views. In a Calcutta Convocation Address, he says:—

"*The real affinities of the people are with Europe and the Future, not with India and the Past.*"

THE VISIT OF MRS. BESANT.

To go back he considers highly detrimental:

"*On the educated Native of India the Past presses with too awful and terrible a power for it to be safe for him to play or palter with it. The clouds which overshadow his household, the doubts which beset his mind, the impotence of progressive advance which he struggles against, are all part of an inheritance of nearly unmixed evil which he has received from the Past.*"

An intelligent Hindu in Madras observed, that so far as the influence of Theosophy extended, it had "put back India half a century."

To aid, in some measure, to counteract the mischief which Mrs. Besant is doing, a small compilation has been issued, entitled, THEOSOPHY EXPOSED; or, MRS. BESANT AND HER GURU. It contains Professor Sidgwick's Report and other *data* for forming an opinion.

How far Mrs. Besant's attempted revival will spread and how long it will last, depends very much on the attitude of the Press. *The Bombay Gazette*, *The Times of India*, and *The Indian Spectator* spoke in just terms of the early movement, and the "scented garlands" of the Western Presidency soon lost their fragrance. Occultism fitly found its permanent headquarters among "The Benighted."

The *Saturday Review's* opinion of *The Theosophist* has been quoted. A volume of Addresses by Colonel Olcott was also reviewed, and pronounced to be "a howling menagerie of mixed metaphors." "A supernaturalism which is a dry rot that can be built upon, which eats out hearts, and incubates satire, and hangs round necks like an incubus, is a very odd agency indeed, and worthy of the rhetoric of Olcott Science." "Theosophy is a mere mixture of the faith in Kitty King, with smatterings of Oriental studies misunderstood and misapplied."*

The *Saturday Review* adds: "We shall be grievously neglecting our duty if we allow such trash to be circulated in India under the name of Science and 'Theosophy!'" Much more is this incumbent upon Indian Journalists.

Under the name of the "WISDOM RELIGION," a trickster, plagiarist, forger, and liar, sought by lying wonders to revive some of the exploded superstitions of the dark ages. A most careful investigation, by competent men, convicted her of imposture,

---

* The article is headed, "Olcott Science." It is quoted in a Madras Paper of April 25th, 1885.

and showed the crass ignorance of herself and her so-called Mahatmas. Mrs. Besant brushes aside all this evidence with "righteous scorn," and with mingled audacity and folly avows her full belief in such a Guru.

It must be admitted that she knows her audience. The average Hindu intellect has been hypnotised, dwarfed into childhood. But more is expected from the leaders of public opinion. Let them give no uncertain sound.

J. MURDOCH.

MADRAS, *December*, 1893.

MRS. BESANT.

THEOSOPHY EXPOSED:

OR,

Mrs. BESANT AND HER GURU.

AN

APPEAL TO EDUCATED HINDUS.

MADAME BLAVATSKY.

FIRST EDITION, 5,000 COPIES.

MADRAS:
THE CHRISTIAN LITERATURE SOCIETY.
S. P. C. K. PRESS, VEPERY.

1893.

THEOSOPHIC GEMS.

Culled from *Isis Unveiled*, written by Madame Blavatsky, with the supernatural aid of the "Brothers," or Mahatmas, and declared to be "minutely correct." See pp. 45-47.

The whole story of the massacre of the children at the birth of Jesus in Matthew was 'bodily taken' from the BAGAVED-GITTA. ii. 199.

The BAGAVED-GITTA contains an account of Vishnu assuming the form of a fish to reclaim the Vedas lost during the deluge. ii. 257.

Maha-Maya, or Maha-Deva, the mother of Gautama Bhudda, had the birth of her son announced to her by Bhôdisât. i. 92.

Opinion of *Isis Unveiled* expressed by Professor Max Müller, Editor of the *Rig-Veda* and of the Sacred *Books of the East* :—

"There is nothing that cannot be traced back to generally accessible Brahmanic or Buddhistic sources, only everything is muddled or misunderstood. If I were asked what Madame Blavatsky's Esoteric Buddhism really is, I should say it was Buddhism misunderstood, distorted, caricatured. There is nothing in it beyond what was known already, chiefly from books that are now antiquated. The most ordinary terms are misspelt and misinterpreted." *The Nineteenth Century.* May, 1893, p. 775.

PREFATORY NOTE.

The following compilation has been suggested by the visit to India of Mrs. Besant.

There is a Latin proverb, *De mortuis nihil nisi bonum*, Of the dead let nothing be said but what is good. Under ordinary circumstances this rule ought to be observed; but when the dead are used to diffuse most pernicious error among millions of the living, the hope of India, the truth ought to be spoken.

Still, it may be said to be unfair to bring charges against the dead who cannot rebut them. They were made in 1884, when Madame Blavatsky was alive, and was publicly challenged to disprove them in a Court of law. (See page 11.)

A careful study of the following papers will show that Madame Blavatsky and her followers are most unsafe religious guides.

The attention of educated Hindus is especially invited to the closing chapter. Instead of accepting what is virtually a godless philosophy, let them hold fast the great truths, that God is our Father in heaven, and that our first duty is to be obedient and loving children. Acknowledging the Fatherhood of God, the Brotherhood of Man follows as a legitimate inference.

J. MURDOCH.

MADRAS, *December*, 1893.

CONTENTS.

		Page
1.	SPIRITUALISM	7
2.	EXPOSURE OF MADAME BLAVATSKY BY THE *Madras Christian College Magazine*	11
3.	REPORT OF THE PSYCHICAL RESEARCH SOCIETY..	12
4.	CRITICAL HISTORICAL REVIEW OF THE THEOSOPHICAL SOCIETY	21
5.	MADAME BLAVATSKY AND HER CHIEF DUPES	37
6.	THEOSOPHIST DOCTRINES	45
7.	DEFECTS OF THEOSOPHY..	53
8.	ORIGIN OF THE THEOSOPHICAL SOCIETY..	60
9.	THE VISIT OF MRS. BESANT	65
10.	GOD OUR HEAVENLY FATHER	93

APPENDIX.

LIST OF PUBLICATIONS 102

The Portrait of Madame Blavatsky is from a photograph by Resta, Coburg Place, Bayswater. That of Mrs. Besant, from a photograph by Sarony.

THEOSOPHY EXPOSED.

1. SPIRITUALISM.

Some account may be fitly given of this system, with which the founders of Theosophy originally started.

Belief in Ghosts.—" Modern Spiritualism," says a writer in the *Encyclopædia Britannica*, " arose from one of the commonest superstitions in the world." Interesting details regarding the different notions entertained of ghosts, or disembodied spirits, will be found in Tylor's *Primitive Culture*. The most troublesome ghosts were supposed to be those of men notorious for their violence during life or of persons who had been murdered.

Faith in ghosts was gradually disappearing among enlightened nations. About seventy years ago, Sir Walter Scott, in his *Demonology and Witchcraft*, could say, " the increasing civilisation of all well-constituted countries has blotted out the belief in apparitions." Their physical causes became understood. Sully says, "Kant observed that the madman is a dreamer awake, and more recently Wundt has remarked that, when asleep, we 'can experience nearly all the phenomena which meet us in lunatic asylums.'"* Some affection of the brain, which in its severer form causes insanity, may, in a milder degree, occasion spectral illusions. The case of Nicolai, a German bookseller, is well known. The following is abridged from his own account :—

"I generally saw human forms of both sexes, but they usually seemed not to take the smallest notice of each other, moving as in a market-place, where all are eager to press through the crowd; at times, however, they seemed to be transacting business with each other. I also saw several times people on horseback, dogs, and birds. I also began to hear them talk: the phantoms sometimes conversed among themselves, but more frequently addressed their discourse to me."†

---

* *Illusions*, p. 182.   † Hibbert's *Philosophy of Apparitions*, pp. 6, 7.

Nicolai's illusions were caused by too much blood. When some was withdrawn by the application of leeches, the illusions began to fade, and at last they dissolved in the air. Hibbert gives an account of different supposed apparitions, arising from excited states of particular temperaments, &c.

Rise of Spiritualism.—Formerly ghosts, for the most part, moved silently in dim twilight, though noisy apparitions were also known. They likewise contented themselves with terrifying people. In 1847-8 they made a new departure, answering questions by means of raps. This first took place in the United States, that land of marvels. Colonel Olcott thus magniloquently describes the new phenomenon:—

"If ever there was a fact of science proved, it is that a new and most mysterious force of *some* kind has been manifesting itself since March 1848, when this mighty modern epiphany was ushered in, with a shower of raps, at an obscure hamlet in New York State. Beginning with these percussive sounds, it has since displayed its energy in a hundred different phenomena, each inexplicable upon any known hypothesis of science, and in almost, if not quite, every country of our globe."[*]

The "inexplicable phenomena" began with the "so-called 'spirit rap.' By these simple signals the whole modern movement called Spiritualism was ushered in."[†] Persons supposed to be able to hold intercourse with spirits were called *mediums*. Answers to questions were denoted by a certain number of raps.

The rappings were so successful that the spirits were encouraged to give other manifestations of their presence. Some mediums claimed to have the "power of floating in and moving through the air, of raising tables from the ground and keeping them suspended, and of performing many other supernatural feats."

The first professed mediums were two young sisters of the name of Fox. They were followed by Davis, the "Poughkeepsie Seer," the Eddy Brothers, Katie King, Dr. Slade, and others too numerous to mention.

---

[*] Addresses, p. 58.   [†] Ibid, p. 61.

Spread of Spiritualism.—The believers in this system *claim* to be fifteen millions strong. This is an exaggeration, but they are numerous. "Man," says *The Saturday Review*, "is naturally prone to superstition, and in his earlier stages of culture will invent the strangest theories to account for the phenomena he sees around him. So much of this old leaven is left in us, that any new doctrine, however preposterous it may be, is sure to find adherents."

It was said of the ancient Athenians that they "spent their time in nothing else, but either to tell or to hear some new thing." Spiritualism has been taken up by many in the same way. Some thoughtful men are drawn to it for a higher reason: "Inquirers who live in constant fear that science is trying to demonstrate the truth of materialism, and to rob them of their dearest hope, that of a future life in the society of their departed friends, turn eagerly to what they think ocular evidence of another existence."*

That there should be so many spiritualists is not surprising. Carlyle, with grim humour, describes the population of the British Islands, about thirty millions, as "mostly fools." Colonel Olcott bears the following testimony to the presence of some of them in India :—

"I can show any of you, if you chose, a bundle of requests for the miraculous cure of physical and mental ailments, the recovery of lost property, and other favours. And, lest my English auditors might be disposed to laugh in their sleeves at Hindu credulity, let me warn them that some of the most preposterous of these requests have come from their own community; some from persons so highly placed that they have asked that their names may be withheld at all hazards." *Addresses*, p. 107.

Reasons for Disbelief in Spiritualism.—The great body of scientific men reject the system for the following reasons :—

1. As a rule these phenomena are exhibited in the presence of 'sensitives,' who are paid for exercising their profession and who prefer to do so in a dark room.

---

* *Encyclopædia Britannica*, Vol. II.

2. As a rule, nothing worth notice has occurred at *séances*,* when competent observers have been present.

3. When strange phenomena have been witnessed, they have often been traced to conscious imposture and *legerdemain*.

4. When conscious imposture does not come in, *unconscious cerebration* and *unconscious muscular action*, supervening on a state of *expectant attention*, are just as deceitful.

5. The received spiritualist theory belongs to the philosophy of savages. A savage looking on at a spiritual *séance* in London would be perfectly at home in the proceedings.

6. The reported doings and sayings of the spirits are trivial, irreverent, useless and shocking.

There is scarcely any literature, not even the records of trials for witchcraft, that is more sad and ludicrous than the accounts of spiritual *séances*.†

Acknowledgments of Trickery.—Mr. Crookes, a noted spiritualist, makes the following admission :—

"In the countless number of recorded observations I have read, there appear to be few instances of meetings held for the express purpose of getting the phenomena under test conditions."‡

Colonel Olcott confesses, "a multitude of sickening exposures of the rascality of mediums,...and the average puerility and frequent mendaciousness of the communications received." "Little by little a body of enthusiasts is forming, who would throw a halo of sanctity around the medium, and by doing away with test conditions, invite to the perpetration of gross frauds. Mediums actually caught red-handed in trickery, with their paraphernalia of traps, false panels, wigs and puppets about them, have been able to make their dupes regard them as martyrs to the rage of sceptics, and the damning proofs of their guilt as having been secretly supplied by the unbelievers themselves to strike a blow at their holy cause !§ The voracious credulity of a large body of Spiritualists has begotten nine-tenths of the dishonest tricks of mediums."‖

---

* Sittings with a view of holding intercourse with spirits.
† Abridged from the *Encyclopædia Britannica*, Vol. II.
‡ Olcott's Lectures, p. 60.
§ These words suggest an application.
‖ Olcott's Lectures, pp. 58, 59, 60.

The foregoing remarks refer only to SPIRITUALISM, properly so called—professed direct intercourse with departed spirits. They do not apply to hypnotism and kindred subjects.

2. EXPOSURE OF MADAME BLAVATSKY BY THE MADRAS CHRISTIAN COLLEGE MAGAZINE.

The early notices of Theosophy in the *Madras Christian College Magazine,* were so mild, that " in some quarters it was exposed to a suspicion of lukewarmness in its opposition to a thoroughly anti-Christian movement. It was even held up by Colonel Olcott as a pattern to others."* Better acquaintance led to a very decided change of policy. The Editor says :—

"So long as the leaders of the Theosophical movement could be spoken of with respect, they received that respect in the pages of this Magazine, and now that we must a different tale unfold, we had rather hold our peace. But our duty to the public which both in its Native and in its European contingents, has been so completely hood-winked, demands that we speak out. What follows is serious matter, quite as serious to us as to Madame Blavatsky. We have weighed the responsibility and resolved to take it up. After satisfying ourselves by every precaution that the sources of the following narrative are genuine and authentic, we have resolved, in the interests of public morality, to publish it."†

Then 43 pages follow, giving full details, showing the real character of the alleged phenomena.

Colonel Olcott mentions above that "mediums caught red-handed in trickery, are able to make their dupes regard them as martyrs, and the damning proofs of their guilt, as having been secretly supplied by the unbelievers themselves to strike a blow at their holy cause." The Theosophists

---

* Vol. II. p. 303.   † Vol II. p. 200.

adopted the same tactics. The letters were alleged to be forgeries; " only a pretext to injure the cause of Theosophy." Madame Blavatsky was challenged to disprove their genuineness in a Court of law; but this she prudently declined.

The Rev. George Patterson, then Editor of the *Christian College Magazine*, deserves great credit for the manner in which the fraud was exposed. The view taken by him may be regarded as also held by the Rev. Dr. Miller, and the other Professors of the Madras Christian College.

To economise space and avoid repetition, details are not given under this head. The principal facts are noticed in the Proceedings of the Society for Psychical Research given below, and in other chapters which follow.

3. REPORT OF THE PSYCHICAL RESEARCH SOCIETY.

This Society was founded in 1882, under the Presidency of Professor H. Sidgwick of Cambridge, author of *The Method of Ethics*, &c. Its object is to make " an organised attempt to investigate that large group of debatable phenomena designated by such terms as mesmeric, psychical, and spiritualistic." Some distinguished men are connected with it. The following Report was written by Professor Sidgwick. It is followed in the Proceedings* by " 2. Account of Personal Investigations in India, and discussion of the Authorship of the " Koot Hoomi" Letters, by Richard Hodgson."

Mr. Hodgson's "Account" occupies 193 pages, and contains " Plan of Occult Room with Shrine and Surroundings," together with *fac similes* of a number of the Letters.

---

* December, 1885. Published by Trübner & Co. Price 4s. 6d.

REPORT OF THE COMMITTEE

APPOINTED TO

INVESTIGATE PHENOMENA CONNECTED WITH THE THEOSOPHICAL SOCIETY.

STATEMENT AND CONCLUSIONS OF THE COMMITTEE.

In May, 1884, the Council of the Society for Psychical Research appointed a Committee for the purpose of taking such evidence as to the alleged phenomena connected with the Theosophical Society as might be offered by members of that body at the time in England, or as could be collected elsewhere.

The Committee consisted of the following members, with power to add to their number:—Messrs. E. Gurney, F. W. H. Myers, F. Podmore, H. Sidgwick, and J. H. Slack. They have since added Mr. R. Hodgson and Mrs. H. Sidgwick to their number.

For the convenience of Members who may not have followed the progress of the Theosophical Society, a few words of preliminary explanation may be added here.

The Theosophical Society was founded in New York in 1875, by Colonel Olcott and Madame Blavatsky, ostensibly for certain philanthropic and literary purposes. Its headquarters were removed to India in 1878, and it made considerable progress among the Hindus and other educated natives. "The Occult World," by Mr. Sinnett, at that time editor of the *Pioneer*, introduced the Society to English readers, and that work, which dealt mainly with phenomena, was succeeded by "Esoteric Buddhism," in which some tenets of the Occult Doctrine, or so-called "Wisdom-religion," were set forth. But with these doctrines the Committee have, of course, no concern.

The Committee had the opportunity of examining Colonel Olcott and Madame Blavatsky, who spent some months in England in the summer of 1884, and Mr. Mohini M. Chatterji, a Brahman graduate of the University of Calcutta, who accompanied them. Mr. Sinnett also gave evidence before the Committee; and they have had before them oral and written testimony from numerous other members of the Theosophical Society in England, India, and other countries, besides the accounts of phenomena published in "The Occult World," "Hints on Esoteric Theosophy," *The Theosophist*, and elsewhere.

According to this evidence, there exists in Tibet a brotherhood whose members have acquired a power over nature which enables them to perform wonders beyond the reach of ordinary men. Madame Blavatsky asserts herself to be a *Chela*, or disciple of these Brothers, (spoken of also as *Adepts* and as *Mahatmas*,) and they are alleged to have interested themselves in a special way in the Theosophical Society, and to have performed many marvels in connection with it. They are said to be able to cause apparitions of themselves in places where their bodies are not, and not only to appear, but to communicate intelligently with those whom they then visit, and themselves to perceive what is going on when their phantasm appears. This phantasmal appearance has been called by Theosophists the projection of the "Astral form." The evidence before the Committee includes several cases of such alleged appearances of two Mahatmas, Koot Hoomi and Morya. It is further alleged that their chelas, or disciples, are gradually taught this art, and that Mr. Damodar K. Mavalankar in particular, a Theosophist residing at the head-quarters of the Society, has acquired it, and has practised it on several occasions. It may be observed that these alleged voluntary apparitions, though carrying us considerably beyond any evidence that has been collected from other sources, still have much analogy with some cases that have come under the notice of the Literary Committee.

But we cannot separate the evidence offered by the

Theosophists for projections of the "Astral form," from the evidence which they also offer for a different class of phenomena, similar to some which are said by Spiritualists to occur through the agency of mediums, and which involve the action of "psychical" energies on ponderable matter; since such phenomena are usually described either as (1) accompanying apparitions of the Mahatmas or their disciples, or (2) at any rate as carrying with them a manifest reference to their agency.

The alleged phenomena which come under this head consist—so far as we need at present take them into account—in the transportation, even through solid matter, of ponderable objects, including letters, and of what the Theosophists regard as their duplication; together with what is called "precipitation" of handwriting and drawings on previously blank paper. The evocation of sound without physical means is also said to occur.

In December, 1884, the Committee considered that the time had come to issue a preliminary and provisional Report. This Report, on account of its provisional character, and for other reasons, was circulated among Members and Associates of the Society for the Psychical Research only, and not published. In drawing up the present Report, therefore, the Committee have not assumed that their readers will be acquainted with the former one. The conclusion then come to was expressed as follows: "On the whole (though with some serious reserves), it seems undeniable that there is a *primâ facie* case, for some part, at least, of the claim made, which, at the point which the investigations of the Society for Psychical Research have now reached, cannot, with consistency, be ignored. And it seems plain that an actual residence for some months in India of some trusted observer—by actual intercourse with the persons concerned, Hindu and European, so far as may be permitted to him—is an almost necessary pre-requisite of any more definite judgment."

In accordance with this view, a member of the Committee, Mr. R. Hodgson, B. A., Scholar of St. John's College, Cambridge, proceeded to India in November, 1884, and after carrying on his investigations for three months, returned in April, 1885.

In the *Madras Christian College Magazine* for September and October, 1884, portions of certain letters were published which purported to have been written by Madame Blavatsky to a M. and Madame Coulomb, who had occupied positions of trust at the head-quarters of the Theosophical Society for some years, but had been expelled from it in May, 1884, by the General Council of that Society during the absence of Madame Blavatsky and Colonel Olcott in Europe. These letters, if genuine, unquestionably implicated Madame Blavatsky in a conspiracy to produce marvellous phenomena fraudulently; but they were declared by her to be, in whole or in part, forgeries. One important object of Mr. Hodgson's visit to India was to ascertain, if possible, by examining the letters, and by verifying facts implied or stated in them, and the explanations of the Coulombs concerning them, whether the letters were genuine or not. The Editor of the *Christian College Magazine* had already, as Mr. Hodgson found, taken considerable pains to ascertain this; but he had not been able to obtain the judgment of a recognised expert in handwriting. Accordingly, a selection of the letters, amply sufficient to prove the conspiracy, was entrusted by the editor (in whose charge Madame Coulomb had placed them), to Mr. Hodgson, who sent it home before his own return. These, together with some letters undoubtedly written by Madame Blavatsky, were submitted to the well-known expert in handwriting, Mr. Netherclift, and also to Mr. Sims of the British Museum. These gentlemen came independently to the conclusion that the letters were written by Madame Blavatsky. This opinion is entirely in accordance with the impression produced in the Committee by the general aspect of the letters, as well as by their characteristic style, and much of their contents.

The Committee further desired that Mr. Hodgson should, by cross-examination and otherwise, obtain evidence that might assist them in judging of the value to be attached to the testimony of some of the principal witnesses; that he should examine localities where phenomena had occurred, with a view of ascertaining whether the explanations by trickery, that suggested themselves to the Committee, or any other such explanations, were possible; and in particular, as already said, that he should, as far as possible, verify the statements of the Coulombs with a view to judging whether their explanations of the phenomena were plausible. For it is obvious that no value for the purpose of the psychical research can be attached to phenomena, where persons like the Coulombs have been concerned, if it can be plausibly shown that they might themselves have produced them: while, at the same time, their unsupported assertions that they did produce them, cannot be taken by itself as evidence.

After hearing what Mr. Hodgson had to say on these points, and after carefully weighing all the evidence before them, the Committee unanimously arrived at the following conclusions:—

(1) That of the letters put forward by Madame Coulomb all those, at least, which the Committee have had the opportunity of themselves examining and of submitting to the judgment of experts, are undoubtedly written by Madame Blavatsky; and suffice to prove that she has been engaged in a long-continued combination with other persons to produce by ordinary means a series of apparent marvels for the support of the Theosophic movement.

(2) That, in particular, the Shrine at Adyar, through which letters purporting to come from Mahatmas were received, was elaborately arranged with a view to the secret insertion of letters and other objects through a sliding panel at the back, and regularly used for this purpose by Madame Blavatsky or her agents.

(3) That there is consequently a very strong general presumption that all the marvellous narratives put forward as evidence of the existence and occult power of the Mahatmas are to be explained as

due either (*a*) to deliberate deception carried out by or at the instigation of Madame Blavatsky, or (*b*) to spontaneous illusion, or hallucination, or unconscious misrepresentation, or invention on the part of witnesses.

(4) That after examining Mr. Hodgson's report of the results of his personal inquiries, they are of opinion that the testimony to these marvels is in no case sufficient, taking amount and character together, to resist the force of the general presumption above mentioned.

Accordingly, they think that it would be a waste of time to prolong the investigation.

As to the correctness of Mr. Hodgson's explanation of particular marvels, they do not feel called upon to express any definite conclusion; since on the one hand, they are not in a position to endorse every detail of this explanation, and on the other hand, they have satisfied themselves as to the thoroughness of Mr. Hodgson's investigation, and have complete reliance on his impartiality, and they recognise that his means of arriving at a correct conclusion are far beyond any to which they can lay claim.

There is only one special point on which the Committee think themselves bound to state explicitly a modification of their original view. They said in effect in their First Report that if certain phenomena were not genuine, it was very difficult to suppose that Colonel Olcott was not implicated in the fraud. But after considering the evidence that Mr. Hodgson has laid before them as to Colonel Olcott's extraordinary credulity, and inaccuracy in observation and inference, they desire to disclaim any intention of imputing wilful deception to that gentleman.

The Committee have no desire that their conclusion should be accepted without examination, and wish to afford the reader every opportunity of forming a judgment for himself. They therefore append Mr. Hodgson's account of his investigation, which will be found to form by far the largest and most important part of the present Report. In it, and the appendices to it, is incorporated enough of the evidence given by members of the Theosophical Society to afford the reader ample opportunity of judging of both its quantity and quality.

There is, however, evidence for certain phenomena which did not occur in India and are not directly dealt with in Mr. Hodgson's Report. Accounts of them will be found at page 382, with some remarks in this by Mrs. H. Sidgwick.

The Report of Mr. Netherclift on the handwriting of the Blavatsky-Coulomb letters will be found at page 381. Extracts from the letters themselves are given in Mr. Hodgson's Report, pages 211—216.

The authorship of the letters attributed to Koot Hoomi, which are very numerous, and many of them very long, is fully discussed in Mr. Hodgson's Report. It may be mentioned here that it is maintained by some that the *contents* of these letters are such as to preclude the possibility of their having been written by Madame Blavatsky. This has never been the opinion of the Committee, either as regards the published letters or those that have been privately shown to them in manuscript. Those who wish to form an independent opinion on the subject are referred to "The Occult World" and "Esoteric Buddhism," which contain many of the letters themselves, and much matter derived from others.

In this connection may be conveniently mentioned what the Committee, in their First Report, called the most serious blot which had then been pointed out in the Theosophic evidence. A certain letter, in the Koot Hoomi handwriting, and addressed avowedly by Koot Hoomi from Thibet to Mr. Sinnett, in 1880, was proved by Mr. H. Kiddle, of New York, to contain a long passage apparently plagiarised from a speech of Mr. Kiddle's made at Lake Pleasant, August 15th, 1880, and reported in the *Banner of Light* some two months or more previous to the date of Koot Hoomi's letter. Koot Hoomi replied (some months later) that the passages were no doubt *quotations* from Mr. Kiddle's speech, which he had become cognisant of in some occult manner, and which he had stored in his mind;

but that the appearance of plagiarism was due to the imperfect precipitation of the letter by the chela, or disciple, charged with the task. Koot Hoomi then gave what he asserted to be the true version of the letter as dictated and recovered by his own scrutiny apparently from the blurred precipitation. In this fuller version the quoted passages were given as quotations, and mixed with controversial matter. Koot Hoomi explained the peculiar form which the error of precipitation had assumed by saying that the quoted passages had been more distinctly impressed on his own mind by an effort of memory than his own interposed remarks; and, that inasmuch as the whole composition had been feebly and inadequately projected, owing to his own physical fatigue at the time, the high lights only, so to speak, had come out; there had been many illegible passages which the Chela had omitted. The Chela, he said, wished to submit the letter to Koot Hoomi for revision, but Koot Hoomi declined for want of time.

The weakness of this explanation was pointed out (in *Light*) by Mr. Massey, who showed (among other points) that the quoted sentences seemed to have been ingeniously twisted into a polemical sense, precisely opposite to that in which they were written.

And more lately (in *Light*, September 20th 1884), Mr. Kiddle has shown that the passage thus restored by no means comprises the whole of the unacknowledged quotations; and, moreover, that these newly-indicated quotations are antecedent to those already admitted by Koot Hoomi, and described as forming the introduction to a fresh topic of criticism. The proof of a deliberate plagiarism aggravated by a fictitious defence is therefore irresistible.

In conclusion, it is necessary to state that this not the only evidence of fraud in connection with the Theosophical Society and Madame Blavatsky, which the Committee had before them, prior to, or independently of, the publication of the Blavatsky-Coulomb correspondence. Mr. C. C. Massey had brought before them evidence which convinced both him and them that Madame Blavatsky had, in 1879, arranged with a medium, then in London, to cause a "Mahatma" letter to reach him in an apparently "mysterious" way. The particulars will be found at page 397.

It forms no part of our duty to follow Madame Blavatsky into other fields. But with reference to the somewhat varied lines of activity which Mr. Hodgson's Report suggests for her, we may say that we cannot consider any of them as beyond the range of her powers. The homage which her immediate friends have paid to her ability has been for the most part of an unconscious kind; and some of them may still be unwilling to credit her with mental resources which they have hitherto been so far from suspecting. For our own part, we regard her neither as the mouthpiece of hidden seers, nor as a mere vulgar adventuress; we think she has achieved a title to permanent remembrance as one of the most accomplished, ingenious, and interesting impostors in history.

4. CRITICAL HISTORICAL REVIEW OF THE THEOSOPHICAL SOCIETY.

A Paper read at the Chicago Psychical Science Congress, by WM. EMMETTE COLEMAN, Member, American Oriental Society, Member Royal Asiatic Society of Great Britain, Member Pali Text Society, etc. Reprinted in the *Chicago Religio-Philosophical Journal.**

During the year 1874, the American Press published many accounts of alleged remarkable manifestations of disembodied human spirits taking place at Chittenden, Vermont, through the mediumship of the Eddy Brothers. That these manifestations were fraudulent—and very shallow trickery at most—has been well established. Various *exposés* thereof have been published by myself and others; and the principal materializing medium, William Eddy, has been detected in fraud on several occasions. Colonel Henry S. Olcott, of New York, spent about two

---

*The following reprint is from an Indian newspaper. It may contain some slight errors. The headings are not in the original.

months at the Eddy homestead in the autumn of 1874, during which time he prepared for publication, in the *New York Graphic*, a series of articles descriptive of the phenomena seen by him. On October 14, 1874, Colonel Olcott first met at Chittenden Madame Helena Petrovna Blavatsky, a Russian woman of good family, who seems to have had from childhood an overweening predilection for the mystical and the marvellous, and who had for many years posed as a spiritualistic medium. A strong friendship sprang up between these two, and they soon became comrades or "chums." Early in 1875, we find Colonel Olcott and Mme. Blavatsky in Philadelphia, assuming to investigate the so-called spiritualistic phenomena manifested in presence of Mr. and Mrs. Nelson Holmes. Certain alleged materializations of John and Katie King, through the Holmes, had a short time before been denounced as fraudulent by Robert Dale Owen; and the confederate who had personated Katie King had made a confession of her guilt. Colonel Olcott published in 1875 a narrative of the investigations of himself and Mme. Blavatsky and they declared that the phenomena were all genuine, and the *exposé* of the Holmeses was due to a conspiracy against them. That the whole of the manifestations through the Holmeses were fraudulent is beyond reasonable doubt. They have been many times caught in the act of trickery; and, being detected in such not long after the publication of Olcott's narrative, Mme. Blavatsky, having accomplished her purpose with them, namely, that of deluding Colonel Olcott into the belief of the possession of remarkable psychic power by her (Mme. B.), publicly repudiated further connection with them.

Early Frauds of the Madame.

Mme. Blavatsky had claimed to be herself a medium for the same John King utilized by the Holmeses, and Olcott has told us of various psychic phenomena seen by him claiming to emanate from John King, and performed through Mme. Blavatsky. It is evident that Mme. Blavatsky and the

Holmeses were in collusion in the production of spurious phenomena palmed off on Olcott as genuine. R. B. Westbrook, LL.D., one of the original officers of the Theosophical Society, stated in *The Religio-Philosophical Journal*, Chicago, Sept. 14, 1889, that Mrs. Holmes had admitted as much, and had stated that Mme. Blavatsky proposed to her a partnership in the " materialization show business," with Colonel Olcott as manager, claiming that she had already so " psychologized him that he did not know his head from his heels." Early in 1875, Mme. Blavatsky sent to General F. J. Lippitt a picture, which she said had been painted for the General by the spirit John King himself. In *Mind and Matter*, Philadelphia, Nov. 27, 1880, was published conclusive evidence, found in Mme. B's room in Philadelphia, that she had herself painted this picture, except certain flowers, etc., which were already on the satin when she procured it. Mme. Blavatsky is known to have fair skill as a painter. Further, Mrs. Hannah M. Wolff, of Washington, D. C., in a published account of her experience with Mme. Blavatsky in 1874, has stated that Mme. Blavatsky having claimed that certain pictures were painted by spiritual power direct, she was watched by three journalists residing in the same house, and they saw Mme. Blavatsky get up in the night and paint them herself. About this time, Mrs. Wolff discovered that the MS. of a book which Blavatsky submitted to her for revision, and which she claimed was her original work, was an almost verbatim translation from a Russian book. In Cairo, Egypt, in 1872, certain spiritualistic phenomena with which Mme. Blavatsky was connected were found out to be fraudulent, and she narrowly escaped personal violence from the enraged populace whom she had deceived. It is also evident that she was in collusion with Eddy Brothers at Chittenden ; as one of the pretended spirits gave her a part of a buckle, said to have been brought by spirit-power from the grave of her father in Russia, whereas it had never been in her father's grave, and she had no doubt carried it with her to Chittenden for the purpose of getting up the sensational display of alleged occultic power in which it subsequently played its part.

The Origin of the Theosophical Society.

So far the outlook is not favourable for genuine psychic phenomena in connection with Mme. Blavatsky. We have had one fraud in Cairo in 1872; two frauds in New York in 1874; three the same year at Chittenden in 1874; four ditto in Philadelphia in 1875. Come we now to the establishment of the Theosophical Society. In the summer of 1875, Colonel Olcott publicly broached the theory that the spiritualistic phenomena were produced by the action of the elementary spirits of earth, air, fire, and water, of the mediæval mystics. At a meeting in Mme. Blavatsky's parlor, Sept. 7, 1875, Mr. George H. Felt having declared that he had the power of controlling and rendering visible the elementary spirits, it was resolved to form a society to conduct research in the department covered by Mr. Felt's alleged discoveries. The first meeting of the Society took place in Nov. 17, 1875, and it was called "The Theosophical Society" for this reason: Webster's Dictionary defines theosophy as supposed intercourse with God and spirits "by physical processes," and as the Society was formed to obtain knowledge of God and spirits "by the aid of physical processes," as stated in its preamble, it was named "Theosophical." Colonel Olcott was elected its President and H. P. Blavatsky, Corresponding Secretary, positions permanently retained by them. Mr. Felt lectured for the Society soon after, but failed to keep his promise —he did not show, as Olcott puts it, "so much as the wag of the tail of a vanishing elemental." From 1875 to 1878 the Society maintained a precarious existence, no psychic phenomena being produced of any moment, and the membership dropping off constantly, until in 1877-78 it was practically dead. In these three years, it added nothing to our knowledge of true psychic science. In 1877 was published Blavatsky's first book, *Isis Unveiled*, which unveils nothing. In it, and in various newspaper articles of H. P. B. (as her friends were wont to call her), and of Colonel Olcott, in 1876-78, were a number of conflicting statements of the producing causes of psychic phenomena

—mere assertions, devoid of all proof, and derived by
H. P. B. from the writings of *Eliphas Levi*, *Paracelsus*,
et al. These theories attributed most of the phenomena to
the action of the already mentioned "elementary" spirits,
now re-christened "elements," and to that of a new class
of "spirits" called "elementaries." The latter were
described as the astral souls of wicked human beings, who
having lost their divine spirit (or immortal soul) before
death, survive for a time in the astral realm as shells or
reliquiæ, gradually becoming disintegrated or annihilated.
The bulk of mediumistic manifestation it was said, is due
to these two classes of spirits; a small part proceeds from
the spirits of the good and pure in the higher life—all this
being dogmatic assertion, without evidence.

THE SOCIETY IN INDIA.

In 1878-79, the Theosophical Society was transferred to
India, as a branch of the Arya Samaj of Swami Dayananda
Saraswati. In 1882 this alliance was broken, and the
Swami denounced Blavatsky and Olcott as tricksters—saying that the phenomena produced by them in India (of
which I shall presently treat) were due to mesmerism, prearrangement, and clever conjuring; and that they knew
nothing of the occult science of the Yogis of old. In 1875
Mme. Blavatsky had claimed to be in communication with
an Egyptian Lodge, called the Brotherhood of Luxor, composed of "Adepts," or "Brothers,"—Masters in Magical
lore; and she also caused Olcott to believe that one or
more of these "Brothers" had accepted him as a pupil,
and that certain communications to him purporting to
come from them, and received by the Colonel through
her, were the veritable productions of these "Adepts."
Olcott asserts that one of them once visited him in his
room in a materialized astral form, and as proof of his
objectivity left with him his head-covering, which the
Colonel retains to this day.

This was no doubt a confederate of H. P. B., employed
for the purpose. It is of a piece with the action of another
confederate of Mme. Blavatsky about this time, of whom

Dr. Westbrook informs us. A woman, strangely attired and veiled, came into the Doctor's house, during a meeting there at which Rev. W. R. Alger, Olcott, and H. P. B., were present, and handed the latter a letter purporting to come from the "Brothers,"—the messenger being presumed to be an elementary. A few months afterward Dr. Westbrook discovered that the presumed elementary was an Irish servant girl, to whom Mme. Blavatsky had promised to pay $5 for the personation of the messenger of the "Brothers." Having failed to get her pay, she confessed the fraud. One of the "Brothers" in communication with Olcott, W. Q. Judge, and others, at this time, was called Serapis; sometimes he was called S. Another one was called M. After removal to India, M.'s name was developed into Morya, a Hindu name. This M., or Morya, was alleged to have been the special guru or teacher of Mme Blavatsky from her childhood; and it is claimed that he also became Olcott's guru after the Madame had brought the two together. Towards the latter part of her stay in America, H. P. B. introduced to Messrs. Olcott and Judge an adept called "The Kashmiri Brother." The most noted of the adepts exploited in later years is called Koot Hoomi Lal Singh. His name was unknown in America; it was first given to Mr. A. P. Sinnett in 1880, as one of the letters of Koot Hoomi has stated—the same letter also stating that he (K. H.) was known in America as "The Kashmiri Brother."

Being attracted to theosophy and Madame Blavatsky in 1880 by certain so-called occultic phenomena performed by the latter, Mr. Allan O. Hume and Mr. A. P. Sinnett conducted a correspondence, in that and following years, with the two alleged adepts, M., or Morya, and Koot Hoomi, principally the last named, said correspondence passing through Mme. Blavatsky as intermediary. The locale of the Brothers was conveniently transferred from Egypt and Kashmir to Tibet, where they were said to reside as Buddhist leaders and teachers. Tibet being inaccessible to Europeans, it was impracticable to interview the adepts in their own land, and they refused to show themselves in India to Mr. Hume and Mr. Sinnett. There have been a few instances where a figure alleged to be that of Koot Hoomi has been seen for a short time in India; it is well established that these were fraudulent impersonations, by confederates of H. P. B. In a short time, the theosophic adepts were identified with the mahatmas, a name applied to the ancient Hindu rishis and sages; and since then they have usually been styled mahatmas. Through repeated questioning, Messrs. Hume and Sinnett obtained from the mahatmas portions of a system of philosophy and religion, called by Koot Hoomi "Esoteric Buddhism," the outlines of which are given in Mr. Sinnett's book of that name.

This book was originally to be written by Mr. Hume, and he commenced to prepare it for the press; but he got disgusted with the contradictions, inconsistencies, falsehoods, and double-dealing manifested by the adepts in their correspondence with him, and he accordingly severed all connection with them and with Mme. Blavatsky. Mr. Sinnett then took up the work, wrote it, and published it; and it is this book in particular that gave theosophy the impetus which it received in Europe and America some eight or ten years ago, and made it for a time the fashionable "fad" with certain classes of minds. Mr. Sinnett's first book, *The Occult World*, published in 1880, was devoted to the phenomena ascribed to Mme. Blavatsky and adepts. In this book, and in theosophic literature generally, the mahatmas are described as the flowering of humanity, perfected human beings, having such command over the forces of nature as to work what are ordinarily regarded as remarkable miracles. They are said to be able to travel instantaneously, in their astral bodies, to any part of the world; they can disintegrate and re-integrate matter at will; can manufacture from the elements material objects, such as flowers, saucers, etc.; can precipitate writing upon paper, even in sealed envelopes; can read the thoughts of men, and have a practical omniscience in all mundane matters. Mme. Blavatsky was said to be an initiate of the adepts, having served a seven years' probation with them in Tibet; and she was herself a partial adept, having power to produce many of the phenomena performed by the fully developed mahatma.

The Indian press in 1880 and subsequent years, published many accounts of marvellous psychic phenomena performed by and in connection with Mme. H. P. B.; and in 1884 the Society for Psychical Research, in London, appointed a Committee to investigate these phenomena. A preliminary report, for circulation among members only was published in that year, containing the evidence of Blavatsky, Olcott, Mohini M. Chatterji, and Mr. Sinnett, and the oral and written testimony of numerous others *in re* said phenomena. This evidence was largely devoted to the alleged apparitions of the mahatmas in their astral form and to the asserted projection of his astral body by Damodar K. Mavalankar, an alleged chela (or pupil) of Koot Hoomi, and co-worker with Mme. Blavatsky. In September 1884, appeared in the *Christian College Magazine, Madras*, the first instalment of the noted Coulomb *exposé* of Mme. Blavatsky and the adepts.

THE COULOMB-HODGSON EXPOSURE.

During the absence in Europe of Mme. Blavatsky and Colonel Olcott, the Board of Control in charge at the Theosophical Head-quarters at Adyar, Madras, had in May, 1884, expelled therefrom M. and Mme. Coulomb. Mme. Coulomb had for several years occupied a position of trust at the Head-quarters, and was in the confidence of, and was a special protegé of Mme. Blavatsky. After expulsion she handed over to the editor of the *Christian College Magazine* some seventy or eighty letters and other documents, mostly in Blavatsky's handwriting, which, if genuine, proved that many of the psychic phenomena of Mme. Blavatsky were certainly produced by fraud, including the writing of mahatmic letters. In view of the *exposé* consequent upon the publication of a number of these letters, a member of the Committee of the Society of Psychical Research, on the invitation and at the expense of Prof. Sidgwick, the

President of the Society, Mr. Richard Hodgson proceeded to India in November 1884, and there conducted a three months' investigation of the whole field of psychic phenomena pertaining to the Theosophical Society. The report of Mr. Hodgson, embodying the results of these investigations, was published by the Society for Psychical Research in December 1885; and it is a masterpiece of honest, faithful, painstaking, accurate, and comprehensive research.

The letters of Mme. Blavatsky submitted by Mme. Coulomb were declared by experts to be unquestionably written by the former; the allegations of forgery, interpolations, etc., set up by H. P. B. and her friends, were shown to be entirely false. More important still, the MSS. of a number of the Koot Hoomi letters were carefully compared by Mr. Hodgson, with the undoubted writing of Mme. Blavatsky and also by two of the ablest experts in handwriting in England; and they were declared by all three to be the work of Mme. Blavatsky. It was also proven that Damodar K. Mavalankar had been a confederate of H. P. B., and that, during her absence in Europe, he had written a number of Koot Hoomi letters, in a handwriting in imitation of the Blavatsky K. H. penmanship, but containing certain peculiarities found in his (Damodar's) ordinary writing. The letters of Morya, or Mahatma M. were also shown to have been written by Mme. Blavatsky.

Evidence that the subject-matter of the mahatma letters contained various peculiarities found in Mme. Blavatsky's own writing was also briefly presented by Mr. Hodgson. These letters having been kindly lent to me, not long ago, by Mr. Hodgson, I made a careful analysis of their contents; and I discovered in them overwhelming evidence that they were, one and all, the work of H. P. B. They teem with plagiarisms, just as do all of Mme. Blavatsky's writing; they abound with errors and absurdities in Sanskrit and Tibetan; they have many contradictions and inconsistencies, blunders and misstatements of similar character to those in her works; and they have a large number of marked chirographic and orthographic peculiarities, which I have never seen anywhere except in the writings of the mahatmas and that of H. P. B. Mr. Hume, in a letter in 1883 to Mme. Blavatsky, the original of which is in my possession, told her that he knew that she wrote all the Morya letters and some at least of those signed K. H. That she wrote all of the letters which he received is beyond doubt. The letters attributed to the mahatmas being proved to have emanated from H. P. B. and Damodar, the powers ascribed to them, and which are claimed in these letters, become mythical, and the adepts themselves are resolved into the fanciful output of H. P. B.'s imagination. The so-called appearances of Koot Hoomi at the Adyar Head-quarters have been shown to be, as a rule, productions of M. Coulomb. He, in a dim light, at a convenient distance, walked about with a dummy head and shoulders attached, to represent K. H. The astral journeys of Damodar were found to be imaginary —his alleged appearances at a distance being due to fraudulent contrivance between him and H. P. B. Numerous occult phenomena were said to have taken place in the "Shrine" at the Adyar Head-quarters. Letters addressed to mahatmas placed therein disappeared, in a short time, and answers thereto were found substituted. A broken saucer placed therein was in a few minutes replaced by one completely whole. It was proven that all this was accomplished by fraud. A secret panel was in the back of the shrine, and an aperture and recess in the wall behind enabled a confederate in the next room (Blavatsky's bedroom) to substitute quickly one letter for another, and a duplicate saucer for the one broken. Dr. Franz Hartmann, a leading theosophist then at Head-quarters, admits that the panel was found in the shrine, and that in order that the telltale shrine might not be examined by Mr. Hodgson and the enemies of the Theosophical Society, it was destroyed by himself, W. Q. Judge, and a Hindu. A common phenomenon with Mme. Blavatsky was the sound of a so-called "astral" bell, apparently heard in the air near her. There is evidence that this was produced by a contrivance concealed under her clothing, and operated by pressure of the arm against her side.

Another common phenomenon was the dropping of mahatma letters, usually from the ceiling and sometimes in the open air. Mr. Hodgson was shown an opening in the ceiling whence the letters were dropped by confederates, while those in the air were projected from trees or other convenient places.

Mr. Hodgson's report minutely examines the different phenomena related in Mr. Sinnett's 'Occult World', and establishes fraud in every instance. The widely published case, in which a lost brooch was returned to Mrs. Hume by Mme. Blavatsky in an occult manner, is easily solved, in view of the evidence that Mme. Blavatsky, had the brooch in her possession a short time before the trick was accomplished. The saucer needed to complete the number required at a picnic, and which was found by digging in the ground at a place indicated by Mme. Blavatsky, is readily explained by the fact that it had been placed where it was found by a confederate, while, as was the case in so many of her tricks, the circumstances and conversation were cunningly led up by Mme. Blavatsky to the production of the miracle.

Her correspondence with Mme. Coulomb proved that prearrangement and fraud were practiced in her tricks with cigarette paper. A torn paper was secreted somewhere by her or one of her confederates. A similar paper was torn in a similar manner, in presence of the one for whom the trick was done, and the Mme. stated that she had sent it occultly to the place where the second paper was hidden. Proceeding to that place, the latter was found, which the dupe supposed to be the same paper that he saw torn.

Professor Elliot Coues at one time investigated theosophy thoroughly, and in 1890 published in the *New York Sun* a scathing exposé of Mme. Blavatsky's career and that of the Society, procured from the editor of the *Christian College Magazine*, the original letters of H. P. B., and other documents obtained by him from Mme. Coulomb, including very important letters of Mme. Blavatsky which have never been published. Professor Coues has permitted me to examine these papers, and I am thus enabled to confirm the truth of what Mr. Hodgson has published there anent.

Plagiarism is a marked characteristic of the writings alike of Mme. Blavatsky and of the mahatmas. In *Isis Unveiled* I have traced some 2,000 passages copied from other books without credit. Her *Secret Doctrine* is permeated with similar plagiarisms. The *Voice of the Silence*, claimed to be a translation by her of a Tibetan work, is a compilation from various Buddhistic and Brahmanical works —a wholesale plagiarism. The *Book of Dzyan*, another bogus translation of an alleged ancient work, is also a compilation from various uncredited sources—all of them 19th century books. I have traced to the books whence copied passages in the writings of the mahatmas in *The Secret Doctrine*; while the letters of the mahatmas to Messrs. Hume and Sinnett contain many passages copied uncredited from books, also traced by me to their sources. A letter to Mr. Sinnett from Koot Hoomi, published in the *Occult World*, was copied bodily, with a few verbal alterations, from an address of Henry Kiddle, published in the *Boston Banner of Light* a short time before K. H. (?) wrote the letter. All the doctrines taught by H. P. B. and the adepts, including minutiæ and details are "borrowed" from the writings of others. There is nothing original anywhere in theosophy, except the distortion, perversion, garbling, and misstatements inherent in its literature, as presented by the mahatmas and Mme. Blavatsky.

Mr. Hodgson shows, in his Report, that among Mme. Blavatsky's confederates was a Hindu usually called Babajee D. Nath, but whose real name was S. Krishnaswami. On September 30, 1892, this Babajee made a confession of his experiences with the theosophical leaders, solemnly declared to be true in the name of Parabrahm and the Hindu scriptures. I have a copy of the confession, and it confirms Mr. Hodgson's conclusions, and reveals a mass of depravity sickening to contemplate. He says he became completely under the influence of H. P. B. and Damodar, and he attested as true whatever they told him. H. P. B. gave him a letter from Koot Hoomi, telling him that he was a chela (pupil) of the mahatmas, and that he must call himself a Tibetan—which he did. When Mr. Sinnett published that he (Babajee) had lived ten years with the mahatmas, he was told by Mme. Blavatsky that he had thus lived in his astral body. Damodar explained to him that the false statements made publicly by him (Damodar) regarding Babajee were made from the occultic standpoint. Babajee says he also signed letters drawn up by Olcott for the purpose. He accompanied Mme. Blavatsky to Europe, and there saw her write mahatma letters, which he found identical with letters received in India as from the adepts. Both she and Damodar could write many different hands. While in Europe, Mohini M. Chaterji and B. J. Padshah independently discovered fraud, and the three proceeded to sift the matter. They found bundles of blue and red pencils, with which the mahatma letters were written, and packs of Chinese envelopes, in which the missives were sent. There were also bundles of Tibetan dresses and caps, used in personating the mahatmas. Mme. Blavatsky's Hindu servant, Babula, and others, used to personate the mahatmas in these costumes. This did not fall to him (Babajee) on account of his short stature. T. Subba Row and A. J. Cooper-Oakely also discovered the fraud, and resigned from the Society, as did M. M. Chatterji, the Gebhards, and others. Numbers of post peons were bribed in India to allow H. P. B. to open the letters, which was done by thin iron rods heated being passed through the flaps of the envelopes. Being opened, mahatma letters in blue or red pencil were inserted, or remarks penciled on the letters themselves. Accompanying his confession, Babajee submitted letters and documents confirming the truth of his statements.

Not long after the Coulomb-Hodgson exposé, Damodar disappeared, and he has not since been seen. It was claimed that he had gone to Tibet, though some assert that he is dead. It is admitted by the theosophical leaders that Damodar was guilty of much trickery and duplicity in mahatmic matters; and in an alleged letter from Koot Hoomi, which Col. Olcott says he received June 7, 1886, the mahatma says that Damodar had taken part in "many questionable doings.... bringing disgrace upon the sacred science and its adepts." As Damodar and H. P. B. worked in conjunction, this is tantamount to confession of H. P. B.'s guilt.

Since the death of H. P. B., Annie Besant and others have received alleged letters from mahatmas, Koot Hoomi and Morya. Who wrote them? In a letter to Annie Besant from M. M. Shroff, Secretary of the Bombay Theosophical Lodge, April 2, 1892, Mr. Shroff says that Brother W. Q. Judge is "strongly suspected of having forged all along letters in the name of the Masters after H. P. B.'s departure. H. S. Olcott, B. Keightley, and Edge are absolutely convinced that Judge forged these letters, and has been duping and deceiving poor Annie!"

In Mrs. Besant's reply of April 22nd, she says, "I know that Col. Olcott has made random statements to that effect (that Judge forged the letters), as he made random statements about H. P. B. committing frauds." In Mr. Judge's reply to Mr. Shroff, in this matter, he says that Olcott should be asked for the proof of the charges against him (Judge), "for he is the one who has given them out and is their sole author." In a letter of Mr. Shroff to Annie Besant, July 15, 1892, he sends copy of a telegram sent by S. V. Edge to B. Keightley, at Darjeeling, May 11, 1892, as follows: "Red Pencil lines business (that is, mahatma letters) have reached Annie's ears. What can be done? Colonel, yourself, must write some conciliatory letters. Look sharp. Reply." Whether Mr. Judge wrote the letters or not, and I have no knowledge there anent save the above-cited opinions of Olcott *et al*, these facts prove that Col. Olcott has distinctly charged Mr. Judge with their production, and that Messrs. Keightley and Edge, the leading theosophists in India at the time, are implicated in the making of this charge. It is a sad commentary upon the universal brotherhood and altruism which the Theosophical Society vaunts as its primary basis of action and endeavour, that the President of the Society should, rightly or wrongly, charge his duly-elected successor to the Presidency with the heinous offence of forging letters in the name of the Holy Masters—the alleged founders and sustainers of the Society, and the fountain-head of all its inspiration and knowledge.

Consequent upon the publication of the Hodgson Report, the production of phenomena was tabood in the Theosophical Society; and since then the occultic marvels of the mahatmas, Mme. Blavatsky, and Damodar have ceased. Save an occasional letter from one or other of the adepts, said to have been received by the theosophic leaders, no sign of their existence, or of the possession by them or H. P. B., of occult power has been given. The psychical fraudulence till then rampant in theosophy was effectually killed by Mr. Hodgson.

It is generally admitted that since the Coulomb-Hodgson exposé, the Hindu theosophists, as a rule, have abandoned faith in Mme. Blavatsky and the mahatmas; and, as is asserted by prominent Hindus in the Society, the Indians remaining in it do so because they regard theosophy as a revival of Hinduism. "The Coulombs," says N. D. Khandalawala, in letter to B. Keightley, Sept. 8, 1890. " may be said to have given almost the death blow to the Theosophical movement in India.' In a letter of H. P. B., sent to India by the hand of B. Keightley in 1890, entitled " Why I do not return to India," and which was suppressed for prudential considerations, the Madame says that since her departure from India "devotion to the Masters.... has steadily dwindled away," and belief in their existence has been shaken in some, and is positively denied by others. "With the exception of Col. Olcott, every one seems to banish the Masters from their thoughts and their spirit from Adyar. Every imaginable incongruity was connected with these holy names, and I alone was held responsible for every disagreeable event that took place." "The Masters and their spirit are virtually banished."

It is significant that the very cream of the theosophical movement has discovered or admitted the practice of fraud in psychic phenomena by H. P. B., Damodar, and others. Prominent among those who have discovered some of the impositions practiced are the following named, all of whom have been more or less active workers in theosophic propaganda. Many of them have quitted the Society in disgust. Some remain in it still. Some, especially among the latter, do not claim that all of the phenomena were fraudulent, but that the genuine were supplemented by the fraudulent: Col. H. S. Olcott, Dr. Franz Hartmann, Allen O. Hume, T. Subba Row, Prof. Elliot Coues, Mabel Collins, Richard Harte, E. Douglas Fawcett, A. J. Cooper-Oakley, C. C. Massey, A. P. Sinnett, Countess Wachtmeister, Anna Kingsford, Dr. George Wyld, Franz and Aline Gebhard, W. T. Brown, Mohini M. Chatterji, Mons. and Mme. Coulomb, M. M. Shroff, Dr. J. K. Daji, Mrs. Emma Hardinge-Britten, Dr. R. B. Westbrook, Mrs. Isabel de Steiger, N. D. Khandalawala, Tookaram Tatya, A. D. Ezekiel, B. J. Padshah, P. R. Venkataram Iyer, and Babajee D. Nath.

In addition, we have now Bertram Keightley and S. V. Edge associated with Olcott in the charges made by him of fraudulent mahatmic writing since the death of H. P. B.

The limitations of this paper would not permit of proof being adduced, in detail, of the statements made. A summary of results could alone be presented. Conclusive proofs, however, of every assertion herein, are in my possession and will be embodied in full in a work I am now preparing for publication, expositive of the true nature of theosophy and its evidences.

Summing up the results of this inquiry, it is seen that the pretensions of theosophy to the possession of a large mass of the most remarkable genuine psychic phenomena of the century, together with the true philosophy of their production and of the nature and causes of all the varied classes of phenomena the consideration of which has devolved upon this Congress, have been proved baseless in whole and in part. A careful examination of the entire circuit of psychic phenomena connected with theosophy, and of the so-called philosophy put forth in the name of the mythical mahatmas, fails to disclose a single genuine psychic fact of value, excepting perhaps the possession and exercise by Mme. Blavatsky of marked hypnotic power on various occasions, in the furtherance of her schemes—"psychological tricks" or "glamour," to use her own language; while, as regards the philosophy, not one new idea or doctrine, commending itself as worthy of serious scientific consideration, has, in my opinion, been presented. From first to last, as far as is concerned the advancement of rational scientific research upon the important problems in present-day psychic manifestations awaiting solution at the hands of science, I am convinced that theosophy has been and is a signal failure; and in the future, as in the past, we can hardly expect from it any light upon the momentous questions engaging the attention of this Congress.

SAN FRANCISCO, CAL.

5. MADAME BLAVATSKY AND HER CHIEF DUPES.

Had the friends of Madame Blavatsky been content to bury her and her system in oblivion, the dead would have been allowed to rest; but when *atheistic folly* is flaunted as *divine wisdom*, it is a bounden duty to speak out plainly. Some account of the "Founders" of Theosophy and their principal coadjutors will be given to show what importance may be justly attached to their assertions. Any new system may also be rightly tested by its apparent fruits in its advocates.

MADAME BLAVATSKY.

The Theosophist, edited by Madame Blavatsky for several years, has as its motto: "There is no Religion higher than Truth." It is asserted that, "The moral standard of the *Theosophist* is TRUTH." On one of the Theosophist banners was blazoned, "There is no Duty higher than Truth." Has she exemplified this great virtue? Instead of that, she is charged with the following breaches of it:—

Trickery.—Some of these are mentioned in the foregoing papers; as, the professed recovery of a brooch, finding a cup and saucer wanted at a picnic, mending a broken saucer, bell sounds in the air, sending cigarettes, letters from Tibet, etc.

Plagiarism.—A single instance of this may first be quoted.

Extract from Mr. Kiddle's Address, delivered August 15th 1880.	Extract from Koot Hoomi's letter to Mr. Sinnett, first published in June, 1881.
"My friends, *ideas* rule the world, and as men's minds receive new ideas, laying aside the old and effete, the world advances. Society rests upon them; mighty revolutions spring from them; institutions crumble before their onward march. It is just as impossible to resist their influx, when the time comes, as to stay the progress of the tide."	"Ideas rule the world; and as men's minds receive new ideas, laying aside the old and effete, the world will advance, mighty revolutions will spring from them, creeds and even powers will crumble before their onward march, crushed by their irresistible force. It will be just as impossible to resist their influence when the time comes as to stay the progress of the tide."

Professor Sidgwick says, "The proof of a deliberate plagiarism aggravated by a fictitious defence is therefore irresistible." (p. 20.)

The above is only one of numberless instances.

Mr. Coleman says:

"In *Isis Unveiled* I have traced some 2,000 passages copied from other books without credit. Her *Secret Doctrine* is permeated with similar plagiarism. The *Voice of the Silence*, claimed to be a translation by her of a Tibetan work, is a compilation from various Buddhistic and Brahmanical works—a wholesale plagiarism. The *Book of Dzyan*, another bogus translation of an alleged ancient work, is also a compilation from various uncredited sources—all of them 19th century books." See p. 32.

Forgery.—The letters attributed to Koot Hoomi were unquestionably forged by Madame Blavatsky, or in her absence by Damodar.

Lying.—*Hints on Esoteric Philosophy*, No. 1., a pamphlet published during her lifetime, "Issued under the Authority of the Theosophical Society," and acknowledged by Mr. A. O. Hume, contains the following:

"Madame Blavatsky's converse is ...... too often replete with contradictions, inaccuracies, and at times apparently distinct misstatements....

"Her memory is undoubtedly impaired, and not unfrequently, I believe, she quite *unconsciously*, in the course of conversation, makes incorrect, if not absolutely false, statements." pp. 68, 69.

The charge of lying is not confined to individual cases; she is accused of "*consciously weaving for years an enormous network of falsehood.*" The case is thus stated by Mr. Sinnett :—

"There is no immediate alternative between the conclusion that her statements concerning the Brothers are broadly true, and the conclusion that she is what some American enemies have called her, 'the champion impostor of the age.' ... Either she must be right, or she has consciously been weaving an enormous network of falsehood in all her writings, acts, and conversation for the last eight or nine years....Pare away as much as you like from the details of Madame Blavatsky's statement on account of possible exaggeration, and that which remains is a great solid block of residual statement which must be either true, or a structure of conscious falsehood."*

Esoteric Philosophy, previously quoted, says :—

"Admitting Madame Blavatsky's indisputably good family connections and rank, I see nothing in this to bar the possibility of deception. The history of imposture shows that every rank, from prince to peasant, has had its impostors." p. 10.

Instead of being truthful, the founder of the Theosophical movement is charged with TRICKERY, PLAGIARISM, FORGERY, and DELIBERATE FALSEHOOD. She fully deserves the epithet applied to her in America, the "CHAMPION IMPOSTOR OF THE AGE."

Some account of her principal dupes will now be given.

COLONEL OLCOTT.

Colonel Olcott claims to be the PRESIDENT-FOUNDER of the Theosophical Society. The Supplement to *The Theosophist*, January, 1881, gives an account of his public life as a

---

* *The Occult World*, pp. 152, 153.

member of the Bar, as an officer in the Army, Secretary of the National Insurance Convention, Agricultural Editor of *The Tribune*, &c. "Although," he says, "I always took an active part in all that concerned my country and fellow-countrymen, and an especially active one during our late civil war, yet my heart was not set on worldly affairs."* Before he met Madame Blavatsky in 1874, he had "ideas that had been the growth of 22 years' experiences, with mediums and circles." He also makes the following candid acknowledgment: "I was in 1874—a man of clubs, drinking parties, mistresses, a man absorbed in all sorts of worldly public and private undertakings and speculations."†

He acknowledges that he was for 22 years a Spiritualist. His own chief characteristic is the "voracious credulity," with which he charges a "large body" of them. (see page 11.)

The single Cock-lane ghost in England, during the time of Dr. Johnson, was a wonder for half a century; but Colonel Olcott claims to have seen, from first to last, "more than 500 apparitions of dead persons." Among these were—

"Americans and Europeans, Africans and Asiatics, Red Indians of our Prairies and white people, each wearing his familiar dress, and some even carrying their familiar weapons." *Lectures*, p. 68.

Colonel Olcott had perhaps the unique experience of *weighing spirits*. To do this correctly, he obtained one of Howe's best Standard Platform Scales. His experiments elicited the remarkable fact that the spirits could vary their weight. "Honto," weighed successively 88, 58, 58, and 65 lbs; "Katie Brink," 77, 59, 52 lbs.‡

He testifies to have seen the following :—
1. Showers of roses made to fall in a room.
2. Letters from people in far countries drop from space into my lap.
3. Heard sweet music, coming from afar upon the air, grow louder and louder until it was in the room, and then die away again out in the still atmosphere until it was no more.

---

* *Lectures*, p. 164. † *Esoteric Philosophy*, pp. 77–78.
‡ *People from the Other World*, p. 487.

4. Writing made to appear upon paper and slates laid upon the floor.
5. Drawings upon the ceiling beyond any one's reach.
6. Pictures upon paper without the employment of pencil or colour.
7. Articles duplicated before my very eyes.
8. A living person instantly disappear before my sight.
9. Jet-black hair cut from a fair haired person's head.
10. Had absent friends and distant scenes shown me in a crystal.
11. In America more than a hundred times, upon opening letters upon various subjects coming to me by the common post from my correspondents in all parts of the world, have found inside, written in their own familiar hand, messages to me from men in India who possess the theosophical knowledge of natural law.

I have not even half exhausted the catalogue of the proofs that have been vouchsafed to me during the last five years as to the reality of Asiatic psychological science. (pp. 73, 74.)

An Accomplice or Dupe?—The Committee of the Psychical Research Society said in their First Report " that if certain phenomena were not genuine, it was very difficult to suppose that Colonel Olcott was not implicated in the fraud." This formed part of Mr. Hodgson's inquiry. He expresses the following opinion :—

"After reviewing the instances I have given of the unreliability of Colonel Olcott's testimony, some readers may be inclined to think that Colonel Olcott must himself have taken an active and deliberate part in the fraud, and have been a partner with Madame Blavatsky in the conspiracy. Such, I must emphatically state, is not my own opinion, though I should be unwilling to affirm that Colonel Olcott may not, by carrying out supposed injunctions of his 'Master,' have improperly contributed, either by word or action, to the marvellousness of certain phenomena. It is clear, for example, from documents in my possession, that the influence of 'K. H.' has been exerted unsuccessfully in the case of another gentleman, for the purpose of strengthening the evidence for an alleged 'occult' phenomenon, and I can well understand that Colonel Olcott may have been induced by the solemn asseverations of his 'Masters' that certain events occurred, to remember incidents which never happened at all; and how much may have been exacted from his blind obedience it is impossible to determine. Further, his capacity for estimating evidence, which could never have been very great, was probably seriously injured before the outset of his Theosophical career by his faith in Madame Blavatsky, who herself regarded him as the chief of those 'domestic imbeciles' and 'familiar muffs' to whom she refers in her letters to Madame

Coulomb; and writing about him from America to a Hindu in Bombay, she characterised him as a 'psychologised baby,' saying that the Yankees thought themselves very smart and that Colonel Olcott thought he was particularly smart, even for a Yankee, but that he would have to get up much earlier in the morning to be as smart as she was. His candour was shown by his readiness in providing me with extracts from his own diary, and the freedom with which he allowed me to inspect important documents in his possession; and he rendered me every assistance in his power in the way of acquiring the evidence of the native witnesses." pp. 310, 311.

Mr. Hodgson expresses the following opinion as to the value of Colonel Olcott's testimony:—

"The testimony of Colonel Olcott himself I found to be fundamentally at variance with fact in so many important points that it became impossible for me to place the slightest value upon the evidence he offered. But in saying this I do not mean to suggest any doubt as to Colonel Olcott's honesty of purpose." p. 210.

The Committee of the Psychical Research Society, " after considering the evidence that Mr. Hodgson laid before them as to Colonel Olcott's extraordinary credulity, and inaccuracy in observation and inference, desire to disclaim any intention of imputing wilful deception to that gentleman." (See page 18.)

Considering that Colonel Olcott was hoodwinked by uneducated farmers like the Eddy Brothers, and even by servant girls into weighing them as spirits, it is not surprising that he should have been deceived by Madame Blavatsky.

Mr. A. P. Sinnett.

Madame Blavatsky's dupes afford an excellent illustration of the remark that scepticism and credulity are often combined. Persons who are too wise to believe in the existence of an intelligent Creator, accept as true the grossest absurdities. This is nothing new. Lecky says in his *History of European Morals:*—

"There existed, too, to a very large extent, a kind of superstitious scepticism which occupies a very prominent place in religious history." Vol. I. p. 179.

"The period when Roman incredulity reached its extreme point had been the century that preceded and the half century that followed the birth of Christ. . . . . This disbelief, however, as I have already noticed, co-existed with numerous magical and astrological superstitions." *Ibid.* p. 390.

"The notions, too, of magic and astrology, were detached from all theological belief, and might be found among many who were absolute atheists." *Ibid.* p. 393.

Mr. Sinnett is author of *The Occult World*, *Esoteric Buddhism*, and other works which principally brought Theosophy before the English public. He swallowed the following with regard to *Isis Unveiled*:—

"In the production of this book she was so largely helped by the Brothers, that great portions of it are not really her work at all. In the morning she would sometimes get up and find as much as thirty slips added to the manuscript she had left on her table over-night.

"The book was written—as regards its physical production—at New York, where Madame Blavatsky was utterly unprovided with books of reference. It teems, however with references to books of all sorts, including many of a very unusual character, and with quotations the exactitude of which may easily be verified at the great European libraries, as foot-notes supply the number of the pages, from which the passages taken are quoted."*

The *Bombay Gazette*, reviewing *The Occult World*, says:—

"The first act of faith required of the disciple of Occult Philosophy is to purge his mind of belief in an imaginary personal God (p. 185)† and all similar 'current superstitions,' (p. 159). This, we may say in passing, is not in all cases so difficult as one might suppose. Our author, at least, as we shall see, had so loose a hold on these venerable beliefs, that a trick with a clock shade was enough to dislodge them, one and all, from his mind." Sept. 24, 1881.

The following opinion is expressed on the book and its author:—

"We have to face the unpleasant fact that the author and one or two others who, like himself, had some claim to be accepted as representatives here of European learning and culture, have subscribed their faith to as ridiculous a scheme of things as ever called itself a philosophy, and that they have done so on the evidence of as patent a series of juggling tricks as ever imposed on the bumpkins at a village fair."

---

* *The Occult World*, pp. 80, 100. † First Edition.

The New York Herald says of Mr. Sinnett, that he "brays with a fatuous ingenuousness and with a good faith that are charming and purely asinine. . . . . There is nothing occult about Mr. Sinnett; he writes himself down clearly as Dogberry."

In the *Nineteenth Century* for June, 1893, Mr. Sinnett attempts to reply to Professor Max Müller's article on "Esoteric Buddhism" in the May issue. He says:—

"On any subject connected with the sacred literature of the East Professor Max Müller writes—for English readers—with great authority. His article therefore on Esoteric Buddhism will, no doubt, have been accepted but too widely as fatal to the system of thought identified with that expression. He finds nothing in the Buddhist books about any interior teaching behind that plainly conveyed, and confidently declares that nothing of the kind exists."

Mr. Sinnett says that the attack "rests chiefly on an unfavourable survey of Madame Blavatsky's career, associated with criticisms of her book *Isis Unveiled*. That was written some years before Esoteric Buddhism was formulated, and Madame Blavatsky was not the writer who formulated that system." Mr. Sinnett forgets his own astounding statement, quoted above, that "in the production of *Isis Unveiled* Madame Blavatsky was so largely helped by the Brothers, that great portions of it are not really her work at all. In the morning she would sometimes get up and find as much as thirty slips added to the manuscript she had left on her table over-night."

Thus both *Isis Unveiled* and *Esoteric Buddhism* profess to rest on the authority of the "Brothers." Do the "Brothers," like "Doctors," differ?

Madame Blavatsky wrote of Colonel Olcott as a "psychologised baby;" that she had so "psychologised him that he did not know his head from his heels." Mr. Sinnett is evidently another of the same type.

The study of the mental condition of Madame Blavatsky's dupes is commended to the Society for Psychical Research. Have they been affected by some hypnotic influence, so as to accept as true what others know to be palpable frauds?

Mrs. Besant.

This lady, now the principal supporter of the movement, will be noticed in a separate chapter.

6. THEOSOPHIST DOCTRINES.

Theosophists have been sailing under false colours. The name *theosophy* is a misnomer. The word is derived from *theos*, God, and *sophos*, wise. The proper meaning is divine wisdom. It was originally used to express a more intimate knowledge of the relation of the soul with God. As will hereafter be shown, the Founders are avowed atheists. Their Theosophy is therefore ATHEOSOPHY, godless wisdom. But the *Chicago Religio-Philosophical Journal* suggests a still better name, BLAVATSKOSOPHY, Blavatsky Wisdom!

Madame Blavatsky's Ignorance.

Before examining Madame Blavatsky's Wisdom, two illustrations may be given of her scholarship which can easily be understood by every educated Hindu.

Her first great work was *Isis Unveiled*, which, according to the account received by Mr. Sinnett, was largely written by the Mahatmas. It has been carefully examined by Mr. W. E. Coleman in a series of Papers which appeared in the *Chicago Religio-Philosophical Journal* in 1889. The following is an extract from the issue of August 31st:—

"The Bhagavad Gita is the gem of Sanskrit literature..... One would think that if there was any Sanskrit book with which Madame Blavatsky would be familiar, not in the original, for she was and is no Sanskritist, but in translation, it would be the Gita. But when she wrote *Isis* she did not even know the name of the book, and was in ignorance of its contents. In a large number of places in *Isis* she speaks of this book which she calls the *Bagaved gitta*. Note the difference in spelling between this and *Bhagavad Gita*. None but a Sanskrit ignoramus would omit the 'h' after the initial 'B,' or spell Gita with two 't's.' There are no such words in Sanskrit as Bagaved and Gitta, (See *Isis Unveiled*, ii. 199, 257, 275, 277, 405.) So much for the name; now for the contents of the book. *I. U.* ii. 199, states that the whole story of the massacre of the children at the birth of Jesus in Matthew was 'bodily taken' from the Bagaved gitta. There is not a word in the Bhagavad Gita about the slaughter of children at the birth of Krishna, to which she refers. *I. U.* ii. 257, states that the Bagaved gitta contains an account of Vishnu assuming the form of a fish to reclaim the Vedas lost during the deluge, and in ii. 405 is found a purported quotation from the Bagaved gitta concerning the deluge. Nothing of this, in any form or manner, is in the Gita. The truth is that Madame Blavatsky has confounded two very different books the Bhagavad Gita and the Bhagavad Purana. The things which she claims to be in the Gita are in the Purana. In another place she twice speaks of the Bhagavatta (ii. 260), the name of which she spells wrongly, using two 't's' in it instead of one. It is plain that Madame Blavatsky had never seen either of these books, the Gita or Purana. Her information concerning and quotations from them were copied from Lewis Jacolliot's writings. He was her standard authority. As is well known, Jacolliot's works are full of forgeries and blunders, utterly worthless productions; and yet he is Madame Blavatsky's principal authority on Hinduism and Sanskrit literature in *Isis*. That work is full of forgeries from Sanskrit works, adopted and copied as truth from Jacolliot.

"A woman who does not know the difference between the Bhagavad Gita and the Bhagavata Purana, and who cannot spell the name of either correctly, and who adopts Jacolliot as her principal authority, is indeed a reliable writer on Hinduism and Sanskrit literature !!"

Numerous other illustrations are given of her ignorance of Hinduism. The following is a similar example so far as Buddhism is concerned :—

"We read in *I. U.* i. 92 that Maha Maya, or Maha Deva the mother of Gautama Bhudda (*sic*) had the birth of her son announced to her by Bhodisat (*sic*) ..... The name Maha Deva is so common in Hindu literature, as an appellation of Shiva, the third member of the Hindu triad or trimurtti, that it would seem that the veriest smatterer in Hinduism should know better than to call Buddha's mother Maha-Deva. Moreover, no woman could be called Maha-deva in Sanskrit. Deva in Sanskrit is masculine; the feminine is Devi; and Gautama's mother Maya is sometimes called Maha-*Devi*; but never *Deva*."

Two leading English newspapers support Mr. Coleman. The *Saturday Review* characterises *Isis Unveiled* as a "mystical jumble." In a review of the work which appeared in the *St. James' Gazette*, July 30th, 1884, Madame Blavatsky's ignorance is represented as astounding. "Almost every page shows this ignorance."

Yet *The Theosophist* says that in this book, through the assistance of the "Brothers," Madame Blavatsky was able to give references to books of all sorts, including many of a very unusual character, "some out of print, and which the author had never read or seen, yet the passages quoted were proved in each case minutely correct." Vol. I. p. 258.

DOCTRINES.

Space permits only the four principal to be briefly mentioned.

1. **Denial of a Personal God.**—By a "personal God" is meant, not an unconscious force, like a steam-engine; but a Being cognizant of His own existence, and acting with intelligence. Colonel Olcott, in a Catechism which he compiled in Ceylon, where he professed to be a Buddhist, says:

"A personal god Buddhists regard as only a gigantic shadow thrown upon the void of space by the imagination of ignorant men." No. 112.

In reviewing *The Theosophical Society*, by the Rev. A. Theophilus, the confession is made: "Now we desire the reader to properly understand that personally we do not at all deny the charge of atheism, the word being used in an orthodox theistic sense." (*Sept.* 1882.)

The following statement is admitted to be "correct:" "Colonel Olcott, as well as Madame Blavatsky, told the Pandit in the presence of several respectable gentlemen that they did not at all believe in the existence of God."† Another lucid explanation is: "The Founders maintain that they *do* believe in the very Divine PRINCIPLE taught in the Vedas; in that *Principle* which is 'neither entity nor non-entity,' but an ABSTRACT ENTITY, which is *no* entity, liable to be described by either words or attributes."†

The "Universal Divine Principle" is thus explained in *Secret Doctrine* :—

"It is that which is dissolved, or the illusionary dual aspect of That, the essence of which is eternally One, that we call eternal, matter or substance, formless, sexless, inconceivable, even to our

---

† *Theosophist*, June 1882, Sup. p. 7.

sixth sense, or mind, in which, therefore, we refuse to see that which Monotheists call a personal, anthropomorphic God." i. p. 545.

The Bombay Gazette quotes from Mr. Sinnett (See page 43):

"The first act of faith required of the disciple of Occult Philosophy is to purge his mind of belief in an imaginary personal God and in all similar current superstitions."

Space does not permit the arguments adduced by some of the greatest men that have ever lived in proof of the existence of God. A summary of the evidence is given in *Short Papers for Seekers after Truth*.* A more complete view will be found in Row's *Existence and Character of God*. (½ An.)

It is true that the "Divine Principle" mentioned above is rather a vague system of *Pantheism*, but *practically* it is *Atheism*. The following words of Row's apply to similar cases :—

"For the sake of avoiding logical difficulties, they admit the existence of a Being whom they designate God, yet their God is one of whom it is impossible to predicate personality or any attribute which we designate moral. As a belief in such a God can exert no influence on the practical life of man, it is precisely the same as if He existed not, for such a Being can stand in no conceivable relation to human life." p. 1.

Man's duty to the "Divine Principle" is nowhere inculcated.

Theosophy, it is true, does not profess to have any creed; but its "Founders" have been virtually propagandists of atheism.

2. **Belief in Mahatmas.**—*Mahátma* means "great-soul." Mr. Sinnett says: "The older Mahatmas are generally spoken of as Rishis; but the terms are interchangeable, and I have heard the name Rishi applied to men now living. All the attributes of the Arhats mentioned in Buddhist writings are described, with no less reverence in Indian literature, as those of the Mahatmas, and this volume might be readily filled with translations of vernacular books, giving accounts of miraculous achievements by

---

* Sold by Mr. A. T. Scott, Tract Depôt, Madras, Price 1 Anna, with postage, 1¼ As.

such of them as are known to history and tradition by name."*

The chief Theosophist Mahatmas are those who assisted Madame Blavatsky in writing that wonderful book, *Isis Unveiled*, in which the quotations are "in each case minutely correct;" and Koot Hoomi, the plagiarist and liar, who imparted to Mr. Sinnett the hallucinations contained in Esoteric Buddhism.

3. **Karma.**—This word comes from *kri*, to do; it means "deeds" or "actions." Bishop Copleston explains it as *act-force*. The following quotation gives a fair account of it :

"Karma is defined as the unerring law of the universe, the law of cause and effect. It is the doctrine of inflexible justice, that a man will reap just what he has sown. We are taught that in the physical and moral worlds alike, cold, relentless laws are in operation. If a man's life be good, he will receive the exact meed of his well-being. If he commit sin, penalty, precise and proportionate, will visit him. Though evil be long unrequited, yet at length retribution will follow. There is no escape. The results of a man's sins dog him from life to life, though centuries intervene. Nothing is forgiven, and nothing is forgotten. The sinner forgets, Karma remembers. It is said of Buddha that he was one day walking with a favourite disciple, when robbers sprang out of a wood and killed the disciple. Buddha made no sign. Then those that stood by said to Buddha, "Why did you not save him?" Buddha replied, "I could not save him; it was Karma. In a former life he killed a man. And though in this life he has been virtuous, Karma has at last overtaken him. The death he once inflicted has to-day returned upon himself."

To a certain extent, the doctrine is true. It is plainly taught in the Christian Scriptures : "Whatsoever a man soweth, that shall he also reap."

But the Buddhist, Hindu, and Theosophist conception is attended with the following difficulties.

Karma is supposed to be endowed with most wonderful influence and qualities. As a judge, its decisions are marked by unerring wisdom, and its awards are inevitably carried out to the letter. They may be stated more in detail as follows :—

---

* *Esoteric Buddhism* p. 8.

1. *It is most wise.*—A judge of the High Court, able to sentence a man to death, needs great wisdom; how much more is this necessary when the award may be heaven or hell for unnumbered ages!

2. *It is inflexibly just.*—A judge may be wise, but he may be partial. Not so with *karma*. It renders to every one exactly according to his deserts.

3. *Its power extends to all worlds.*—Through it a person is born in one of 84 lakhs of births in this world, in the world of the gods, or in one of the hells.

4. *It extends to all time.*—Its memory never fails. A man may be in the enjoyment of happiness for millions of years on account of some supposed merit, but at the end of that period he may be born in the lowest hell for some crime in a former birth.

5. *It is unalterable.*—The highest gods have no power to avert its effects; they are themselves subject to *karma*.

6. *Its object is good.*—To punish vice and reward virtue, is an aim of the noblest kind.

What is it that is supposed to possess these high attributes? A mere name, something that has no existence. What power is there in an action itself to reward or punish, millions of years after it was performed?

As a rule, there must be some one to give the rewards or punishments due to men's actions. Thus a man is engaged to do a certain work for which he is to receive wages. The work done is the man's *karma*: the wages to be received is the *phala* or fruit. But how is he to receive this *phala*? Is it to be received from the *karma*? No. It must be given by some one able and willing to bestow it. Suppose a thief steals many thousand rupees, will he be punished without the intervention of other persons? Were any person to say that for the purpose of punishing the criminal no judge is necessary, that by demerit of the crime itself the man would be flogged without any one flogging him, would any person of common sense believe him? And if such an assertion cannot be received as true respecting the affairs of this world, can similar assertions be received as true respecting the other world?

If, instead of *karma*, we read God, all becomes plain. He is eternal; His sway extends over all worlds. He possesses all power, omniscience, justice, and goodness. But to ascribe such attributes to a mere word is folly. A living intelligent Being is required.

Karma does not explain the origin of things. Before there could be merit or demerit, beings must have existed and acted. The first in order could no more have been produced by *karma* than a hen could be born from her own egg.

The limitations of the doctrine will be mentioned under another head.

4. **Re-incarnation.**—Before noticing this, a brief account may be given of the three principal *lokas*, or worlds, according to information supplied to Mr. Sinnett by Koot Hoomi :—

"1. *Karma loka;* 2. *Rupa loka;* and 3. *Arupa loka;* or in their literal translation and meaning—1, world of desires or passions, of unsatisfied earthly cravings—the abode of 'Shells' and Victims. of Elementaries and Suicides ; 2, the world of forms—*i.e.*, of shadows more spiritual, having form and objectivity, but no substance ; and 3, the *formless* world, or rather the world of no form, the incorporeal, since its denizens can have neither body, shape, nor colour for us mortals, and in the sense that we give to these terms. These are the three spheres of ascending spirituality in which the several groups of subjective and semi-subjective entities find their attractions." *Esoteric Buddhism*, p. 82. Ed. 1883.

The course of re-incarnation has thus been summarised according to Esoteric Buddhism :—

There are seven planets, through which man passes by successive re-incarnations in the progress of his evolution. These seven planets have each evolved seven races, and these seven races each seven sub-races.

Thus we have 7 planets × 7 races × 7 sub-races, that is $7 \times 7 \times 7 = 343$ stages of existence, and as each man and woman has been twice incarnated in each age we have $343 \times 2 = 686$ as the number of re-incarnations man has had in the seven planets, and, as I understand, this process has been performed seven times in the "spiral" evolution of the planets. We thus have $686 \times 7 = 4,802$ as the number of existences a human soul has in its progress towards a final Nirvana.

Three of these seven planets are the Earth, Mars, and Mercury ; the four others are of so refined a material as to be invisible.

At all his 4,802 deaths man passes into a paradise of happiness and rest, a "world of effects," the average life there being probably 8,000 years between each re-incarnation. Thus the life of man in this world of effects, which is called Devachan, is $4,802 \times 8,000 = 38,416,000$ years. This seems a very long time, but in a conversation I had on the subject, (1) I was informed that although the Brothers were shy as to giving exact quotations in figures, it was yet understood that the probable duration of a finished soul on the planets was more like 70,000,000 years.

Who is the authority for such statements? Koot Hoomi, *i.e.*—Madame Blavatsky.

Mr. Coleman has carefully compared *Isis Unveiled* and *The Secret Doctrine*. In the *Chicago Religio-Philosophical Journal* for August 1893, he points out numerous contradictions between the two books, and concludes as follows:—

"Many other radical contradictions between the two books might be cited, but those on these three cardinal points in theosophy will suffice. The doctrines of reincarnation, the septenary constitution of man, and the nature of elemental spirits are three of the most fundamental constituents of Blavatskyite theosophy; and upon all three the exact opposite is taught in one book to that which the other inculcates. Does this not demonstrate the worthlessness of both as authorities, and the untruth of the oft-repeated claims of Madame Blavatsky that her teachings are those of the all-knowing mahatmas, the sole depositaries of Divine Wisdom on this planet? Is this not evidence conclusive that all her theories are the results of her own cogitations and eclectic plagiarisms from other writers, and that the whole of her writing and teaching about the Himalayan adepts, the Tibetan Koot Hoomi and his coadjutors, is 'absolute fiction,' devoid of any foundation in truth? The entire scheme of theosophy is due to the active brain of Helen P. Blavatsky, its bases and nearly all of its details being borrowed by her from the writings of other authors—a compilation of the grotesque and the *bizarre* from a variety of sources."

To the above may be added the opinion of the eminent scholar, Professor Max Müller, Editor of the *Rig-Veda* and of the "Sacred Books of the East." Referring to Madame Blavatsky's writings he says:—

"There is nothing that cannot be traced back to generally accessible Brahmanic or Buddhistic sources, only everything is muddled or misunderstood. If I were asked what Madame Blavatsky's Esoteric Buddhism really is, I should say it was Buddhism misunderstood, distorted, caricatured. There is nothing in it beyond what was known already, chiefly from books that are now antiquated. The most ordinary terms are misspelt and misinterpreted."*

7. DEFECTS OF THEOSOPHY.

The greatest of Teachers says: "*A corrupt tree bringeth forth evil fruit. Do men gather grapes of thorns or figs of thistles?*" It has been proved incontestibly that the founder of Theosophy was for years "consciously weaving an enormous network of falsehood," while her professed maxim was, "There is no Religion higher than Truth."

It must be admitted that, except among the more enlightened Hindus, this will not weigh much against Madame Blavatsky. The late Maharaja of Travancore said: "see how blandly and unconcernedly the epithet 'liar' is taken by an average countryman of our own!" When Madame Blavatsky's conduct was exposed, the Madras correspondent of the *Pioneer* wrote:—

"I have been told by some highly intelligent men who have joined the Society, 'After all what does it matter? Supposing there have been some tricks and some tac-a-tack business, they were only done in order to attract persons who would not join unless they had some visible manifestations. The tricks have nothing to do with the object of the Society, which is a revival of pure religion.'"

On the other hand Bishop Copleston says:

"The qualities most charming to the Indian mind are gentleness and calmness. It is to an exhibition of these qualities in a high degree that we can attribute with the greatest probability the personal influence of Gotama the Sakyan." *Buddhism*, p. 97.

Let Madame Blavatsky's conduct be tested in this respect. Colonel Olcott says for her and himself:—

"We two Founders profess a religion of tolerance, charity, kindness, altruism, or love of one's fellows; a religion that does not try to discern all that is bad in our neighbour's creed, but all that is good, and to make him live up to the best code of morals and piety he can find in it." *Addresses*, pp. 202-203.

---

* *Nineteenth Century*, May 1890. p. 775.

The contrast between the profession and practice of the "Founders" provoked an indignant letter, signed *Aletheia*,* which appeared in the *Theosophist*, of which the following are extracts:—

"We all realise that, suddenly attacked, the best may, on the spur of the moment, stung by some shameful calumny, some biting falsehood, reply in angry terms. But what defence can be offered for the deliberate publication, in cold blood, of expressions, nay sentences, nay entire articles, redolent with hatred, malice, and all uncharitableness?

"Think, now, if the Blessed Buddha, assailed, as he passed, with a handful of dirt by some naughty little urchin wallowing in a gutter, had turned and cursed, or kicked the miserable little imp, where would have been the religion of Love and Peace?

"But this is the kind of demonstration of Buddha's precepts that the Founders of our Society persist in giving to the world. Let any poor creature, ignorant of the higher truths, blind to the brighter light, abuse or insult, nay, even find fault with them,— and lo, in place of loving pity, in lieu of returning good for evil, straightway they fume and rage, and hurl back imprecations and anathemas, which even the majority of educated gentlemen, however worldly, however ignorant of spiritual truths. would shrink from employing." June, 1882.

A Religion from such "Founders" cannot be expected to be of a high character.

The following are some of the defects of Theosophy:

1. **Its Virtual Atheism.**—Taking the word *God* to mean the Supreme intelligent Being, "the Founders of Theosophy," as already shown (see page 47) are *avowed* atheists. Like Buddhism, their system is, to use the words of Oldenberg, "a proud attempt to create a faith without a God, to conceive a deliverance in which man delivers himself." But they may be said also to profess a vague form of pantheism. It has been shown that this is *virtual* atheism. The belief in an ENTITY which is practically a NONENTITY makes no difference.

Atheism is opposed to the general consent of mankind in all ages. Cicero says: "There is no people so wild and savage as not to have believed in a God, even if they have

---

* Probably written by MR. A. O. HUME; who is now receiving such an ovation in India.

been unacquainted with His nature." Socrates, the wisest of the Greeks, has an interesting dialogue in support of this truth. Sir Isaac Newton was one of the greatest scientists that ever lived. His conclusion is:—

"This most beautiful system of the sun, planets, and comets, could only proceed from the counsel and dominion of an intelligent and powerful Being."

Sir William Thomson, now Lord Kelvin, is President of the Royal Society in London, the highest position a scientist can occupy in England. Addressing some of the most learned men in Europe, he said:—

"Overpowering proofs of intelligence and benevolent design lie around us; and if ever perplexities, whether metaphysical or scientific, turn us away from them for a time, they come back upon us, with irresistible force, showing to us, through Nature, the influence of a freewill, and teaching us that all living beings depend upon the ever-acting Creator and Ruler."

One great difference between a bad and a good lawyer is that the former cannot grasp the whole of a case. He dwells upon one small point, while he overlooks the far stronger arguments on the other side. So it is with atheists.

A parent punishes his child for wrong-doing. For this he is to be praised rather than blamed. Most of the suffering in the world is caused by men breaking God's laws, and the pain is intended to teach them to reform. In this life also people are so bound up together that the innocent child often suffers from the misdeeds of a parent. Granting, however, that there is a residuum of misery which we cannot explain, we should set against this the innumerable proofs of intelligent design, intended, on the whole, to promote our happiness.

"It is a fine observation of Plato in his *Laws*," says Fleming, "that atheism is a disease of the soul before it becomes an error of the understanding." It is generally found among proud dogmatists, not among humble earnest searchers after truth. "A scorner seeketh wisdom and findeth it not."

Milton, the celebrated English poet, thus expresses the feelings which should be called forth by a survey of Creation :—

> "These are Thy glorious works, Parent of good,
> Almighty, Thine, this universal frame,
> Thus wondrous fair; Thyself how wondrous then!
> Unspeakable, who sittest above these heavens
> To us invisible, or dimly seen,
> In these Thy lowest works; yet these declare
> Thy goodness beyond thought, and power divine."

Addison, one of the most distinguished English prose writers, thus expresses the gratitude which should be awakened towards God for His preserving care :—

> When all Thy mercies, O my God!
>   my rising soul surveys,
> Transported with the view, I'm lost
>   in wonder, love, and praise.
> O how shall words, with equal warmth,
>   the gratitude declare
> That glows within my ravish'd heart!
>   but Thou canst read it there.
>
> Thy Providence my life sustained,
>   and all my wants redrest,
> When in the silent womb I lay,
>   and hung upon the breast.
> To all my weak complaints and cries
>   Thy mercy lent an ear,
> Ere yet my feeble thoughts had learn'd
>   to form themselves in prayer.
>
> Unnumbered comforts to my soul
>   Thy tender care bestowed,
> Before my infant heart conceived
>   from whom these comforts flowed.
> When in the slipp'ry paths of youth
>   with heedless steps I ran:
> Thine arm, unseen, conveyed me safe,
>   and led me up to man:

Through hidden dangers, toils, and deaths,
  it gently cleared my way;
And through the pleasing snares of vice,
  more to be feared than they.
When worn with sickness, oft hast Thou
  with health renewed my face;
And when in sin and sorrow sunk
  revived my soul with grace.

Through every period of my life
  Thy goodness I'll proclaim:
And after death, in distant worlds,
  resume the glorious theme,
When nature fails, and day and night
  divide Thy works no more,
My ever grateful heart, O Lord,
  Thy mercy shall adore.

George Eliot, one of the greatest English writers of recent times, says that to form a high character we need "Something to *reverence*, something to *love*." Cicero rightly calls God, *optimus, maximus*, the best and greatest. Who is more entitled to our reverence and love?

Coleridge thus describes atheism:—

"The owlet atheism
Sailing on obscene wings across the moon,
Drops his blue-fringed lids and shuts them close,
And, hooting at the glorious sun in Heaven,
Cries out, "Where is it?""

Christianity teaches that the *first and great commandment, is to love God with all our heart.* The greatest poet of Southern India says:—

"What is the fruit that human knowledge gives,
If at the feet of Him, who is pure knowledge,
Due reverence be not paid?"

Where is this duty inculcated by Madame Blavatsky? The commandment, calculated to have a most beneficial influence on the character, is totally ignored. This is the first and greatest defect of Theosophy.

2. **No Prayer.**—Colonel Olcott says in his *Addresses:* "The Founders of the Theosophical Society do not pray." (p. 119). They are not illustrations, either intellectually

or otherwise, of the advantages of such a course. It must however, be admitted that they are carrying out their principles logically, for it is useless to pray to a Being who does not exist or to an Entity who is practically a nonentity.

In opposition to this, Nature herself teaches us to pray. A Buddhist, when asked why he prayed, replied, "Because I cannot help it." Some Sinhalese before they go to sleep say, "May God protect;" a Burmese in distress cries, "Lord, help me!" Tennyson says:—

"For what are men better than sheep or goats
That nourish a blind life within the brain,
If, knowing God, they lift not hands of prayer
Both for themselves and those who call them friend?"

3. **No Pardon of Sin.**—Theosophists have adopted the Buddhist doctrine of *Karma*, which teaches that neither in heaven nor in earth can man escape from the consequences of his acts. The Gospel of Theosophy, the "glorious truth," according to Colonel Olcott, to be proclaimed "through a sin-burdened world," is that

"Eternal, immutable law punishes the slightest moral sin as certainly as it does every physical sin; and, that as man creates his own destiny, so *he* must be his own Saviour and Redeemer, and can have no other." *Addresses,* p. 38.

Under the head of *Karma* (page 49) it is admitted that Christianity also teaches the general truth that men must reap as they sow, but it is stated to have its limitations. It is a natural law that severe disease should end in death; but a skilful physician intervenes, and the patient may recover. As a general rule, the punishments decreed by law must be inflicted; but the sovereign reserves to himself the right of pardoning if he sees sufficient reason.

Karma, according to Buddhists and Theosophists, is somewhat like fate, an unintelligent force to which there can be no appeal; but it is different if the world is governed by God.

Men instinctively believe in the forgiveableness of sin, and instinctively pray for pardon. An earthly king can pardon an offender; why should this prerogative be denied to the King of kings?

It is admitted that the great problem is how to combine mercy and justice. Christianity sees the difficulty, and points out the solution. Space does not permit details. The reader is referred to *Short Papers for Seekers after Truth,* pp. 70—77.

4. **No Helps to Holiness.**—The *Christian Patriot* justly remarks, "The greatest defect in Theosophy is its being destitute of the ethical element." (Nov. 30th, 1893). This is not surprising. Truthfulness and love are the chief of the cardinal virtues. How could they be inculcated by Madame Blavatsky?

The *Indian Mirror*, some years ago, had the following remarks :—

"O limed soul that struggling to be free
Art more engaged!"

"In these words, Shakespeare, ever true to nature, faithfully depicts the condition of the sinner's soul struggling to be delivered from vicious habits. Are we not all conscious of that state of mind in which the more we try to cut through the fetters of sin, the more inextricably are we enchained?"

Even Colonel Olcott feels the difficulty in some measure. Referring to "SELF" he says,

"This is the coward, the traitor, the despot. the bigot, the swinish sensualist, the lump of egotism. This Self is the serpent coiled beneath the flowers of life. This is that which stifles all good and noble aspirations, and which makes the Rights of Man as a whole ruthlessly sacrificed to the base greed of the individual man." p. 100.

How often have even good men to say in the evening :—

"The day is gone, its hours have run,
And Thou hast taken count of all
The scanty triumphs grace hath won—
The broken vow, the frequent fall."

Among the last words of Buddha to his followers were, *Attasaraná viharatha,* Be your own refuge. Man is to gain salvation by himself and for himself alone. Such also is the teaching of Theosophy.

Christianity likewise says, "Work out your own salvation with fear and trembling," but divine help is offered. A Father's hand is held out to keep us from falling.

5. **Denial of the Fatherhood of God implies denial of the Brotherhood of man.**—According to Theosophy, we have no Father in heaven; we are all independent units, without any relation to each other. The Bible says, " Have we not all one father? hath not one God created us?"

> " Children we are all
> Of one Great Father, in whatever clime
> His providence hath cast the seed of life;
> All tongues, all colours."

We should regard each other as brethren, belonging to the same great family, with God as our Father in heaven. Nominal Christians, it must be confessed, in many cases show as little of this brotherly spirit as the "Founders" of Theosophy; but this is not the fault of Christianity.

---

8. ORIGIN OF THE THEOSOPHICAL SOCIETY, AND ITS COURSE IN INDIA.

The "President-Founder" of the Society says, "On the 17th November, 1875, I had the honor of delivering in the City of New York, my inaugural address as President of the Theosophical Society." Its course was by no means smooth. In his first Indian lecture, Colonel Olcott admits that during the Society's four years of activity in America, there were "foes all about, public sentiment hostile, the press scornful and relentless:" "the press has lampooned us in writing and pictorial caricature." (p. 1), Colonel Olcott was ridiculed as the "Hierophant;" Madame Blavatsky was called "the champion impostor of the age."* The *New York Sun* thus "chaffed" the "President-Founder":—

"While the 'Hierophant' was still a resident of the Eighth Avenue, he had full faith in the capacity of an industrious Theosophist to attain through contemplation, initiation, and a strictly vir-

---

* *The Occult World*, p. 152.

tuous life the power of defying and overcoming what are generally accepted as the laws of nature. He believed in levitation, for example, but when we invited him to illustrate his faith by stepping out of an upper window of the *Tribune* tall tower, he was fain to admit that this was a height of adept science which he had not yet attained and to master which a journey to the Himalayas was necessary."

The above proposal was made to the "Hierophant" before he went to India. The same journal gives the following amusing account of the breach between the "Founders" and Swami Dayanand Saraswati:—

THE WAR IN INDIA.

About three months ago we printed a letter from Mr. H. Burzurgee of Bombay attacking the good faith of Hierophant Olcott and his venerated female companion. Documents were submitted showing that the American Hierophant and the Russian woman approached the Swami with professions of the utmost humility and reverence. "Permit us to give you the name of our Teacher, our Father, our Chief," the Hierophant wrote to the Swami. "We will try to deserve by our actions so great a favour. We await your orders and will obey." But it is alleged that after the Hierophant and the Russian woman had profited by the Swami's instructions—presumably after they had learned all that he had to teach—they went back on that reverend Pandit. They spoke derisively of the Swami Dayanand Saraswati: they repudiated him and his society, the Arya Samaj; they denied that they had ever recognized him as their "spiritual germ;" they forswore allegiance; they even assumed to set up for themselves, and to intimate that a Madison Avenue or Eighth Avenue theosophist stood as near the fountain-head of adept lore as any early Aryan whoever—the Swami Dayanand or any body else. It was at this stage of the controversy that the venerable Swami publicly denounced Hierophant Olcott and his Russian companion as ".... and ....* jugglers.."....

But the *New York Sun* was chiefly interested to know how far the President-Founder's power had been increased by his visit to the Himalayas:—

The question that really interests the American friends of the Hierophant is entirely apart from any personal controversy between him and the venerable Pandit to whom he turned a few years ago for instruction in practical magic. Has the Hierophant made any progress in miracle-working since he left New York? Has he

---

* Epithets omitted in this extract.

become an adept in the inmost mysteries? ... To the results of the Hierophant's journey to India and his proposed studies with the Swami Dayanand Saraswati, we looked forward with interest.

Well, the Hierophant has made the journey, and has so far completed his studies in Yoga Science that he feels himself able to set up for as good a man as the Swami. Has he learned to work miracles? If so, by returning to New York and demonstrating his powers by a public exhibition he can render extraordinary service to the cause of truth. But if he carries out the intention which he announces, that is to say, if he concludes " to live and die in India," we cannot see that we are much better off than we were before he sailed for the antipodes. *August* 20, 1882.

The "Hierophant" and his "venerated female companion," laughed out of New York, according to the phrase of Mr. Thomas, a former ally, took a "header," and turned up in India. The field was wisely chosen, for the Hindus, among their 64 arts and sciences, include the following:—

12. The science of prognosticating by omens and augury.
14. Science of healing, which may include restoration to life of the dead, the reunion of sovered limbs, &c.
15. Physiognomy, chiromancy, &c.
36. The art of summoning by enchantment.
37. Exorcism.
38. Exciting hatred between persons by magical spells.
41. The art of bringing one over to another's side by enchantment.
42. Alchemy and chemistry.
44. The language of brute creatures from ants upwards.
47. Charms against poison.
48. Information respecting any lost thing, obtained by astronomical calculations.
50. The art of becoming invisible.
51. The art of walking in the air.
52. The power of leaving one's own body and entering another lifeless body or substance at pleasure.
56. Restraining the action of fire.
57. The art of walking upon water.
58. The art of restraining the power of wind.
62. The art of preventing the discovery of things concealed.
63. The art by which the power of the sword or any other weapon is nullified.
64. The power of stationing the soul at pleasure, in any of the five stages.*

---

* Winslow's *Tamil Dictionary*, p. 258.

ORIGIN OF THE THEOSOPHICAL SOCIETY.

The first Theosophist party landed at Bombay on the 14th February, 1879. It consisted of Colonel Olcott, Madame Blavatsky, and two English members recently admitted. During the year they were joined by M. and Madame Coulomb, old Egyptian acquaintances of Madame Blavatsky.

On account of the "Russian scare," they were at first coldly received; but this suspicion was afterwards removed. In 1880 Colonel Olcott and Madame Blavatsky visited Ceylon, where they acknowledged themselves to be Buddhists. This created a great sensation among the Sinhalese, and they had almost a royal progress. A tour during the same year in North India, was so successful, that Colonel Olcott could report that "Things are booming along splendidly."

The first visit of the "Founders" to Madras was in April 1882, when they met with a cordial welcome. During the same year Colonel Olcott made his third visit to Ceylon, where he is said to have "healed more than fifty paralytics, in each case using the name of Lord Buddha."* Still more remarkable for its "astounding cures" was the Bengal tour in 1883. Colonel Olcott's Acting Private Secretary reports 2812 cases treated.

Towards the close of 1882, the head-quarters were transferred from Bombay to Madras.

During the absence of Colonel Olcott and Madame Blavatsky in 1884, the *Madras Christian College Magazine* exposed the real character of the so-called phenomena. This gave a great blow to the cause which gradually declined.

Mr. Sydney V. Edge, Assistant Secretary at the Madras Head-quarters, in an article entitled, "The Hour of India's Need," in the issue of *The Theosophist* for September, 1892, thus frankly described the state of things at that time :

"Of cheap encouragement we have had more than enough, but honeyed speeches, flattery, and empty show will not suffice. We may appreciate the kind remarks, the flattering speeches of the

---

* *The Theosophist*, April, 1883, p. 159.

Hindus, we feel honoured when decked with wreaths and garlands, it is pleasant to hear one's praises sung, no doubt, but—we are not deluded. We none of us feel in our inmost hearts, that a large concourse at the railway-station, numbers of smiling faces, their owners all anxious to say something pleasant, a crowded lecture-hall, a flattering vote of thanks; I say, we none of us feel that any of these can, in the least degree, be taken as a criterion of the well-being of Theosophy, or of the real earnestness and deep-rooted sincerity of our Hindu Brothers. It is easy to flutter people, far pleasanter to sing the praises of the Hindu nation, to speak of their spirituality and freedom from Western vices, their simplicity of habit and simple manners of life, but it is far more important, and better becomes an earnest Theosophist, to speak the truth and to tell of things as we find them, even at the risk of personal unpopularity. Better for us all to realise exactly how we stand, as regards our duty to ourselves, our fellow Theosophists, and the world at large, than to delude ourselves by outward show, and to accept pretty sayings and empty talk instead of solid work and definite results." pp. 744, 745.

Money is the crucial test of interest in a movement. What does Mr. Edge say under this head?

"Our records we can scarce look at without a blush of shame, for they are stained with a series of broken promises and unfulfilled obligations. Donations offered voluntarily and never paid, assurances of help never realised, promises to study our books and to work for our movement never fulfilled, such are some of our wounds; and they never heal, for they are constantly opened afresh. The Head-quarters' staff may write till their pens drop in sheer weariness from their hands; lecturers may travel from branch to branch, exhorting members to be true to their cause; the word Theosophy may become known throughout the length and breadth of the land; but it will never be practicably realised while Hindus sleep in idleness as they do now." p. 747.

The above is only a repetition of what Colonel Olcott experienced at Bombay. At his last Bombay Anniversary Address on January 12th, 1882, he said :—

"We have got beyond the preliminary stage of polite phrases on both sides. You know just how we keep our promises, and we know what yours are worth. The scented garlands Bombay brought us in February 1879, withered long ago, its complimentary speeches of welcome long since died away in the air." (p. 116).

9. VISIT OF MRS. BESANT.

This lady is perhaps the most important adherent that Madame Blavatsky ever made. The story of her life is pathetic. She is a mournful example of scepticism and credulity. The numerous phases of unbelief and belief through which she has passed will be briefly described. The authorities are chiefly her own writings and a sympathetic sketch of her life, by Mr. Stead, which appeared in the *Review of Reviews* in October, 1891.

Early Life.—Mrs. Annie Besant's maiden name is Wood. Her father was cousin to Lord Hatherley, a Lord Chancellor of England. Her mother was Irish. She was born in 1847, so that she is now about 46 years of age. Her father died when she was only 5 years old. The bereavement made, in one night, her mother's raven hair white as snow. Mrs. Wood wished to give her son a University education. To provide the means she removed to Harrow, where she opened a boarding house for boys attending the Harrow school. Her daughter for a short time was brought up among the boys—as good a cricketer and climber of trees as any of them.

Miss Marryat, a rich benevolent lady, offered to educate Annie free of charge. Mrs. Besant thus acknowledges her obligations to her: "No words can tell how much I owe her, not only of knowledge, but of that love of knowledge which has remained with me ever since as a constant spur to study."

Miss Marryat "visited the poor, taking help wherever she went, and sending food from her own table to the sick." She was an earnest Christian. Annie learnt passages from the Bible and hymns for repetition. She was also made to teach in the Sunday School, for Miss Marryat said, "it was useless to learn, if we did not try to teach those who had no one to teach them."

After leaving Miss Marryat, the young girl returned to Harrow. There, besides reading, "she was devoted to archery and croquet, and danced to her heart's content with the junior masters, 'who could talk as well as flirt.'" Her mother seems afterwards to have removed to London.

A High Church Christian.—In every religion there are differences of opinion. Hinduism has its six schools of philosophy, some of them much opposed to one another, yet all acknowledging the Vedas. Men differ in politics as well as religion. Some Englishmen almost worship Mr. Gladstone; others regard him as one of their country's worst enemies. When men exercise their judgments, there must, on numerous questions, be differences of opinion. All Christians, properly so called, agree on many of the most important points. They believe in the same God, the same Saviour, and accept the Bible. The short statement of belief, usually called the Apostles' Creed, is generally acknowledged.

The two principal divisions of Christians are Roman Catholics and Protestants. Besides disagreeing on some important points of doctrine, they differ in Church Government and ritual. The Roman Catholic Church acknowledges the Pope of Rome as its head; its cathedrals are often splendidly decorated; various rich vestments are used in its public religious services. Among Protestants the Pope is not recognised, and the tendency in worship is towards simplicity.

The Church of England is properly Protestant; but there is a section within it having a leaning, more or less, towards the Church of Rome. This is called the *High Church* party, to which Mrs. Besant belonged. When a young lady in London, she delighted in making ornaments and arranging decorations for a Mission Chapel. She also there made the acquaintance of the Rev. Frank Besant, who helped at the Mission, and supported himself as under-master of Stockwell Grammar School. In 1867, when about 20 years of age, she married him. The first pamphlet which she published was a little tract, Roman Catholic in its tone, which insisted upon the virtue of fasting.

Theist.—Two or three years after her marriage, atheistic thoughts began to trouble her; but before noticing them an account may be given of her path to Theism. Doubts about some Christian doctrines weighed heavily upon her mind. In distress, as a last resource, she went to Dr. Pusey, considered the leader of the High Church party. He did not understand her case, and the interview did no good. She then became a Theist for a time, and attended the lectures of Moncure Conway.

Atheist.—It was the sickness of her infant daughter that first led Mrs. Besant to become an atheist. The child had a severe attack of whooping cough, so that her life was despaired of. The cry broke from the mother's lips, "How canst Thou torture a baby so? Why dost Thou not kill her at once and let her be at peace?...My mother's heart rose up in rebellion against this Person in whom I believed, and whose individual finger I saw in my babe's agony."

From the earliest times the existence of so much suffering in the world has perplexed good men. As already mentioned, most of it arises from the breach of God's laws, natural and moral. As there are, on the other side, numberless proofs of God's wisdom and goodness, the most thoughtful men are content to wait for an explanation till they get "within the veil, within the veil!"

A few further remarks on this point may be offered, chiefly based on Row's *Christian Theism*. It is so ordained that poison kills and fire burns. The Creator does not interfere miraculously with the operation of such laws. A poison given by mistake from the loving hand of a wife kills as surely as if administered by an enemy. Unless the laws did act thus, the whole course of human life would become a scene of hopeless confusion.

If the people in the East end of London, or anywhere else, spend their money on strong drink, does their misery disprove God's existence?

But far greater minds than Mrs. Besant's have recognised the value of the "discipline of sorrow," properly used. Millions upon millions of Christians can say with the Psalmist, "It is good for me that I have been afflicted." How many have been led by the sickness and death of their children to think of a world where there is no more pain or death! The trial may be so severe that the afflicted one may cry out in agony, "Father, if it be possible, let this cup pass from me," but faith enables the words to be added, "Nevertheless, not as I will, but as Thou wilt," or the exclamation, "Though He slay me yet will I trust in Him." Some of the noblest characters have thus been formed. Christians acknowledge that even the "Captain of their salvation was made perfect through suffering." But unsanctified sorrow has a very different effect.

As Mrs. Besant's "Theism melted into Atheism, prayer was gradually discontinued as utterly at variance with any dignified idea of God, and as in contradiction to all the results of scientific investigation."*

A further result is given in her own words:

"God fades gradually out of the daily life of those who never pray; a God who is not a providence is a superfluity; when from the heavens does not smile a listening Father, it soon becomes an empty space, whence resounds no echo of a man's cry." *Review of Reviews.* p. 360.

The Preface to *My Path to Atheism* concludes as follows:

"The path from Christianity to Atheism is a long one, and its first steps are very rough and very painful; the feet tread on the ruins of broken faith, and the sharp edges cut into the bleeding flesh; but further on the path grows smoother, and presently at its side begins to peep forth the humble daisy of hope that heralds the spring-tide, and further on the roadside is fragrant with all the flowers of summer, sweet and brilliant and gorgeous, and in the distance we see the promise of the autumn, the harvest that shall be reaped for the feeding of man."

The way in which this glorious change is to be brought about is thus explained in her *Constructive Rationalism* :—

"Full of hope, full of joy, strong to labour, patient to endure, mighty to conquer, goes forth the new glad creed into the sad grey Christian world; at her touch men's faces soften and grow purer, and women's eyes smile instead of weeping; at last, at last, the heir arises to take to himself his own, and the negation of the usurped sovereignty of the popular and traditional God over the world developes into the affirmation of the rightful monarchy of man." pp. 177, 178.

---

* Preface to *My Path to Atheism*.

The golden age is to begin when man, the rightful lord of the universe, takes the throne usurped by God! Most persons will rather be reminded of Byron's words:

"Lord of himself—that heritage of woe!"

When women embrace atheism; so opposed to their naturally religious disposition, they are generally blatant. A poet of last century describing society in his time says:

"Here a female atheist talks you dead."

Both by her voice and her pen, Mrs. Besant was an active fellow-worker with Mr. Bradlaugh. A gentleman in Ceylon says that he heard her stand in the Hall of Science, in London, with a watch in her hand saying, "If there be a God, let Him strike me dead in five minutes."

Malthusian.—Malthus held that population tends to increase faster than the means of subsistence, and therefore urged that an increase of population should be checked. Mr. Bradlaugh and Mrs. Besant printed and circulated a work proposing certain means for this purpose. While it was fitted to answer this end, experience showed that it might also be used to render seduction and adultery safe from discovery, although such was not the intention of the publishers. The book became the subject of a public prosecution. It was afterwards replaced by one from the pen of Mrs. Besant, of a somewhat similar character.

Materialist.—Materialism denies the existence of spirit, and maintains that there is but one substance—matter. It naturally accompanies atheism. Death ends all. "As calmly as the tired child lies down to sleep in its mother's arms, and passes into dreamless unconsciousness, so calmly does the Rationalist lie down in the arms of the mighty mother, and pass into dreamless unconsciousness on her bosom."*

Mrs. Besant had now reached the bottom: afterwards there was some ascent.

Spiritualist.—About 1889, Mr. Stead says:

---

* *My Path to Atheism*, p. 175.

"Mrs. Besant, with Mr. Herbert Burrows, began to investigate at regular séances the phenomena of spiritualism. I never attended any of these séances, but heard a good deal about them, especially on one occasion when the table announced the death of a well-known clergyman, who obligingly mentioned the place of his death, and sent messages to his bereaved relations. Fortunately the table lied, as tables will, for the clergyman shortly after turned up alive and well."*

Theosophist.—Madame Blavatsky's *Secret Doctrine* was given to Mrs. Besant to review. Mr. Stead says:

"She asked me for an introduction to Madame Blavatsky, which I gladly gave her, little dreaming that I was thereby providing H. P. B. with an heir and successor. Such, however was the case. Mrs. Besant brought to the Theosophists a zeal and an enthusiasm at least equal to that of H. P. B., while she placed at their service a reputation for absolute sincerity and an eloquence superior to that of any living platform orator. She espoused Madame Blavatsky's cause with the devotion of a neophyte. She sat at her feet learning like a little child all the lore of the Mahatmas; she was obedient in all things; and when at last Madame Blavatsky passed away, Mrs. Besant was instinctively recognised as her only possible successor." *Review of Reviews,* Vol. IV. p. 366.

Mr. Stead rightly describes her attitude towards Madame Blavatsky: "She sat at her feet like a little child learning all the lore of the Mahatmas." The grand article of her creed now is, *I believe in Madame Blavatsky.* This is shown by her answers at Tanjore.

Do you believe in what the Theosophists call " phenomena"?
"I do believe in phenomena. They were shown me and their reasons were explained to me by Madame Blavatsky who was my *Guru,* and I understood them as the results of psychic development."
Q. Have you seen a Mahatma?
A. I have.†

Anti-Malthusian.—In 1891 Mrs. Besant refused to print any more or to sell the copyright of the "Law of Population." "Having taken this step, it is right to take it publicly, and to frankly say that my former teaching was based on a mistaken view of man's nature, treat-

---

* *The Review of Reviews,* Vol. IV. pp. 365, 366.
† *Madras Mail,* Dec. 2, 1893.

ing him as the mere product of evolution instead of as the spirit, intelligence, and will without which evolution could not be." *Review of Reviews*, August, 1891, p. 143.

Anti-Materialist.—For years Mrs. Besant taught that death ends all. This is now condemned as pernicious error. Re-incarnation is substituted on the authority of Madame Blavatsky and the Mahatmas.

Present Religious Belief.—In *Why I became a Theosophist*, Mrs. Besant says, the first thing Theosophists learn is "that every idea of the existence of the supernatural must be surrendered. . . *There is no such thing as a miracle.*" p. 17.

"The next matter impressed on the student is the denial of a personal God." Elsewhere she says: "As regards belief in a personal God, I have nothing to say different from what I wrote years ago. The concept of a personal God is as impossible to me now as it was then."

She calls herself a Pantheist:

"In Theology, Theosophy is Pantheistic. 'God is all and all is God.' It is that which is dissolved, or the illusionary dual aspect of That, the essence of which is eternally One, that we call eternal, matter or substance, formless, sexless, inconceivable even to our sixth sense, or mind, in which, therefore, we refuse to see that which Monotheists call a personal anthropomorphic God." (*Secret Doctrine*, i. 545).*

Tennyson, in *In Memoriam*, expresses the following opinion of Pantheism:—

"That each, who seems a separate whole
    Should move his rounds, and fusing all
    The skirts of self again, should fall
Remerging in the general soul,
Is faith as vague as all unsweet:
    Eternal form shall still divide
    The eternal soul from all beside."

---

* *Review of Reviews*, Vol. iv. p. 366.
* *Why I became a Theosophist*, p. 18.

Esoteric Hinduism, *alias* Theosophy.

The Mahatmas, that is Madame Blavatsky, revealed to Mr. Sinnett what he calls *Esoteric* Buddhism. *Esoteric* comes from *esō*, within. It was originally applied to the private instructions of Pythagoras, the ancient Greek philosopher, which were not explained to the general body of his disciples. The teaching of the latter was called *exoteric*, from *exō*, outwards. Max Müller, Monier Williams, Rhys Davids, Oldenberg, and others, are acquainted only with *exoteric* Buddhism. Mr. Sinnett was honoured to be the instrument of making known to the world its *esoteric* doctrines.

Mrs. Besant delivered a lecture in the Hindu College, Tinnevelly, which has been summed up as follows:—

1. The Hindu theosophy is the best of all philosophies.
2. The Hindus are the wisest of all nations.
3. The Sanskrit language is the best of all languages.
4. Western civilization, with all its discoveries in science, is nothing compared with Hindu civilization.
5. All that is best in the west has been borrowed from India.

It is added:

"All these statements, of course, were received by the audience with the loudest cheers."

Franklin tells us that when he was a boy, he was flattered into turning a grindstone to sharpen an axe, till his hands were blistered. When it was completed, all the thanks he got were, "Now, you little rascal, you've played the truant; scud to school or you'll have it." The lesson he drew from it was that when people flatter you, they have "some axe to grind." Mrs. Besant is an astute woman, and does not spend her powder and shot in vain. What is her object in her outrageous flattery of the Hindus?

It is to persuade them that Theosophy is the most perfect form of Hinduism, revealed in these last days by the Mahatmas, in Madame Blavatsky's *Secret Doctrine*, etc.

It may be asked why have the Hindus so long been acquainted only with the exoteric doctrines of Hinduism?

Mrs. Besant explains the cause. In a lecture at Trichinopoly, as reported by the correspondent of the *Madras Standard*, (Dec. 8) she makes the following astounding statement, no doubt on the authority of the Mahatmas:

"That the present Vedas are not the whole, but that thousands of Slokas have disappeared. That the latter have not been lost, but they have been taken away by the gods knowing that in the *Kali Yuga* India would be brought under foreign yoke, and fearing that the ignorant foreigner would desecrate the sacred science."

This assertion is simply a fiction of her Guru, a convicted liar and trickster. It is totally opposed to fact. At an early period before the foot of foreign invader had touched the soil of India, every verse, every word, every syllable of the Rig-Veda had been carefully counted. The number of verses varies from 10,402 to 10,622 according as a few hymns are included or left out; the number of *padas*, or word is 153,826; that of the syllables, 432,000.*

Theosophy, which Mrs. Besant tries to palm off as "pure and entire" Hinduism, is chiefly derived from a French book of magic by a writer who calls himself Eliphas Levi, from Paracelsus, and other medieval mystics. See *Koot Hoomi Unveiled*, by Arthur Lille, Member of the Royal Asiatic Society. Mr. W. Emmette Coleman is preparing a work (see page 36) in which this will be substantiated by full quotations.

Mrs. Besant asserts that "Western civilization is as nothing compared with Hindu civilization." The reader is referred on this point to the learned work of his countryman, Mr. R. C. Dutt, the translator of the Rig-Veda into Bengali: *Civilization in Ancient India*, 3 Vols., published by Thacker, Spinck & Co., Calcutta. An abridgment has been issued in England. An abstract will be found in the following pamphlet: *Civilization, Ancient and Modern Compared*. (1½ As. Post-free, 2 As.)

Sir H. S. Maine said truly in a Calcutta Convocation Address: *The real affinities of the people are with Europe and the Future, not with India and the Past.*

---

* Max Müllers' *Ancient Sanskrit Literature*, p. 221.

Madame Blavatsky and Mrs. Besant, the Guru and Chela, both Charlatans.

Charlatan comes through the French from the Italian word, meaning a *quack*, which, in its turn, comes from a word meaning *to chatter like birds*. It denotes, "one who prates much in his own favour and makes unwarrantable pretensions to skill." How far does this apply to the Guru and Chela?

It has been shown that Madame Blavatsky and the Mahatmas, when they jointly produced that ponderous work in two thick octavo volumes called *Isis Unveiled*, could not even spell correctly the name of the Bhagavad Gita (See page 4). Every educated Hindu can judge of this. Another illustration, from Manu's Code, may be given of crass ignorance which applies to both Guru and Chela. This may be taken as what the lawyers call a *test case*.

The Guru.—Madame Blavatsky, after admitting that she had made no study of Hindu Law, pronounces this positive judgment :—

" I regard the Hindu Law as almost the embodiment of justice; and the Hindu religion as the ideal of spiritual perfectibility. When any one points out to me in the existing canon, any text, line, or word that violates one's sense of perfect justice, I instinctively know it must be a later perversion of the original *Smriti*."*

Mr. Siromani, of the College of Pandits, Nadiya, in his *Commentary on Hindu Law* (p. 15) says, " The Code of Manu is not only the most important of all the legal codes, but it is regarded as almost equal in holiness to the Vedas."

It is allowed that the Code has its excellencies, especially considering the time at which it was composed ; but a few quotations will show how far it may be considered as " almost the embodiment of justice."

Some extracts are first given about *Women*—a most important subject, having a vast influence over the destinies of India.

---

* Letter to Dowan Ragunath Rao on Widow Marriage, quoted by Rev. A. Theophilus.

It is true that women are commanded to be honoured, but it is for a selfish reason :—

"Women are to be honoured and adorned by fathers and brothers, by husbands, as also by brothers-in-law who desire much prosperity." III. 55.

"Therefore they are ever to be honoured at ceremonies and festivals, with ornaments, clothes, and food, by men who desire wealth." III. 59.

How Women may be punished, etc.—The rule has been quoted, both in Calcutta and Madras, "Strike not, even with a blossom, a wife guilty of a hundred faults." Manu, the highest authority, lays down a very different law.

A WIFE, son, slave, pupil, and own brother should, when they have committed faults, be beaten with a cord or a bamboo cane.

But on the back of the body (only), never on a noble part : if one should smite them on any other part than that, he would incur the sin of a thief. VIII. 299, 300.

Evil Qualities of Women.—"The bed, the seat, adornment, desire, wrath, deceitfulness, proneness to injure, and bad morals, Manu (the Creator) ordained for women." IX. 17.

No Religious Duties for Women.—For women there is no separate sacrifice, nor vow, nor even fast; if a woman obeys her husband, by that she is exalted in heaven. V. 115.

No religious ceremony for women should be (accompanied) by *mantras* (except marriage),—with these words the rule of right is fixed; for women being weak creatures, and having no (share in the) *mantras*, are falsehood itself. So stands the law. IX. 18.

Look at the Code as the "embodiment of JUSTICE" between man and man :—

Thus, whatever exists in the universe is all the property of the Brahman; for the Brahman is entitled to all by his superiority and eminence of birth. I. 100.

Certainly (the king) should not slay a Brahman even if he be occupied in crime of every sort; but he should put him out of the realm in possession of all his property, and uninjured (in body). VIII. 380.

Sudras created for servitude.—But a Sudra, whether bought or not bought, (the Brahman) may compel to practise servitude; for that (Sudra) was created by the Self-Existent merely for the service of the Brahman. VIII. 413.

A Brahman may take possession of the goods of a Sudra with perfect peace of mind, for, since nothing at all belongs to this (Sudra) as his own, he is one whose property may be taken away by his master. Book VIII. 417.

If a (man) of one birth assault one of the twice-born castes with virulent words, he ought to have his tongue cut out, for he is of the lowest origin. VIII. 270.

The atonement for killing a Sudra is the same as for killing the following animals:

On killing a cat, an ichneumon, a daw, or a frog, a dog, a lizard, an owl, or a crow, he should practise the observance (ordained for) killing a Sudra. Book XI. 132.

The National Congress is to meet shortly at Lahore. Manu's Law with regard to public assemblies should be "observed to the letter :"

"If a low-born man endeavours to sit down by the side of a high-born man, he should be banished after being branded on the hip, or (the king) may cause his backside to be cut off." VIII. 281.

Mrs. Besant may say with Madame Blavatsky that the above are "later perversions of the original *smriti*." The whole Code was translated from the Sanskrit by Sir William Jones, Chief Justice of Bengal, a distinguished Sanskrit scholar, who may be said to have first made Sanskrit literature known to Europe. What does he think of the book? In the Preface to his translation he says :—

"It is a system of despotism and priestcraft, both indeed limited by law, but artfully conspiring to give mutual support, though with mutual checks; it is filled with strange conceits in metaphysics and natural philosophy, with idle superstitions, and with a scheme of theology most obscurely figurative, and consequently liable to dangerous misconception; it abounds with minute and childish formalities, with ceremonies generally absurd and often ridiculous; the punishments are partial and fanciful, for some crimes dreadfully cruel, for others reprehensibly slight; and the very morals, though rigid enough on the whole, are in one or two instances (as in the case of light oaths and of pious perjury) unaccountably relaxed."*

So much for Manu's Code being the "EMBODIMENT OF JUSTICE!"

---

* See *Manava-Dharma Sastra: Who wrote the Code of Manu?* Pice Paper on Indian Reform, ¼ Anna. Sold by Mr. A. T. Scott, Tract Depôt, Madras.

The Chela.—Mrs. Besant has made a grand discovery—*why India has fallen so often under a foreign yoke!*

The correspondent of *The Hindu* gives an account of one of her lectures in the Kumbakonum Town Hall, "full to suffocation." The following is an extract:

"Mrs. Anne Besant said that India was a mighty country so long as the dictates of Manu the Legislator were observed to the letter; but when the spirit of his dictates was forgotten by them, hordes after hordes of foreign conquerors swept over the land and subjugated it." Dec. 7th, 1893.

Instead of that, the effect has been *just the opposite*. Manu's Code is the grand support of Caste, well described by Sir H. S. Maine in *Ancient Law*, as "THE MOST DISASTROUS AND BLIGHTING OF HUMAN INSTITUTIONS." Professor Bhandarkar says: "The caste system is at the root of the political slavery of India."

The Romans had a maxim, "Divide and conquer." The Brahmans acted upon the same principle. By splitting up the people into numerous sections, they more easily retained their supremacy. "A nation divided against itself," is the proper description of the Hindu race. Hence India has become the easy prey of foreign invaders. Sir Lepel Griffin thinks it would be politic on the part of the British Government to encourage caste.

Pandit Sivanath Sastri, after enumerating other evils connected with caste, says:

"9. It has made the country fit for foreign slavery by previously enslaving the people by the most abject spiritual tyranny."

Yet Mrs. Besant poses as the advocate of this blessing of ancient Hindu civilization.

Every educated Indian can form an opinion as to the above test case, and can decide whether the Guru and Chela are justly or unjustly termed *charlatans*.

In confirmation of the above may be adduced the following description of Mrs. Besant by "one of the most brilliant *alumni*" of the Madras University, after hearing three lectures by her at Tanjore. Acknowledging that she has "a splendid physique, and a voice that can be heard distinctly to the furthest end of the biggest hall," he adds :—

"She is extraordinary in being able to speak for a full hour and a half with the same fervour, real or feigned, from beginning to end. But her eloquence is of the stump-oratory order, likely to take with the ignorant many who delight in 'sound and fury,' and not with the cultured few. She is extraordinary in being able to build up the most daring conclusions on the flimsiest basis of facts, with the aid of the crudest hypotheses and the most far-fetched analogies. Her self-assurance is something extraordinary. She can talk glibly of the Vedas, the Upanishads, the Puranas, the Sthula and Linga Sariras, the Akasa, and all the endless terminology of Hindu Philosophy and Religion as if she were a profound scholar of these subjects. But beneath all this show of knowledge, one can detect that it is from a cursory perusal of translations and magazine articles that the little modicum of information she possesses has been gathered. It is therefore extraordinary to find that on this slender substratum of information she can pose as a leader of Hindu thought, and pretend to have crossed the ocean to instruct the Hindus and revive their ancient greatness."

Mrs. Besant has had very long experience in public speaking, and has great art in managing the audiences to which she has been accustomed; but well educated, thoughtful men will agree with the foregoing opinion.

Theosophists on Indian University Education.

Colonel Olcott pours contempt on the so-called scientific studies of the Indian Universities. The heads of students are "crammed with a terrible lot of poor stuff;" they are "baked dry in the scholastic ovens of Elphinstone College" (p. 124.). He says:

"The science we have in mind is a far wider, higher, nobler science than that of the modern sciolists. Our view extends over the visible and invisible, the familiar and unfamiliar, the patent and the occult sides of Nature. In short, ours is the Aryan conception of what science can be and should be, and we point to the Aryans of antiquity as its masters and proficients. Young India is a blind creature whose eyes are not yet open, and the nursing mother of its thought is a bedizened goddess, herself blind of one eye, whose name is modern science." (pp. 83, 84.)

Colonel Olcott directs the students to whom to go for the genuine article :—

"Pshaw! Young man of the Bombay University, when you have taken your degree, and learned all your professors can teach you, go to the hermit and recluse of the jungle, and ask *him* to prove to you where to begin your real study of the world into which you have been born!" (p. 149).

The exact *spot* where it is to be found is also clearly indicated :—

"If you drag the depths of the ocean of human nature, if you study the laws of your own self, if you turn the eye of intuition to those profounder depths of natural law, where the demiurgic Hindu Brahma manages the correlations of forces and the rhythmic measures of the atoms, and the eternal principle of motion, called by the Hindu Parabrahm, outbreathes and inhales universes,—*there* will the golden key of this Ineffable Knowledge be found." (p. 129).

Mrs. Besant indulges in similar rant.

"Western civilization, with all its discoveries in science, is nothing compared with Hindu civilisation."

Madras students were the most demonstrative of the whole community in their admiration of Mr. A. O. Hume during his recent visit. What reception will those whose "heads have been baked dry in the scholastic ovens" of the Madras Colleges give to Theosophists who so highly appreciate their attainments?

The Flattery of Theosophists.

"A man that flattereth his neighbour spreadeth a net for his feet."

Hindus are peculiarly susceptible to flattery. Skilful flatterers can induce them to part with almost anything. It is the expectation of flattery that makes them squander such large sums on marriages. The Theosophists knew the weak point of the Hindus.

When Colonel Olcott began the movement in India, he employed the most fulsome flattery, and, like Mr. Facing-both-ways, suited it to his audience. The following are some specimens:

INDIA.

"I recognise the Vedas as the earliest of extant religious writings, the repository of the highest thought of archaic man, the spring source of all subsequent philosophies." p. 125.

"This magnificent Eastern philosophy." p. 11.

"This fact, that we deny that the sun of Aryan wisdom has set to rise no more, is the one memorable feature of this evening's festivity. Brothers, that glorious sun will again shine over the world through the gloom of this Kali-Yug." p. 19.

CEYLON.

"Buddhism is the religion of one-third of the human race. The philosophy of Gautama is so profound, so comprehensive, so sounds the depths of human nature, opens up such limitless vistas of progressive unfolding of the spiritual out of the physical—that it deserves the first attention of the student of Theosophy." p. 34.

Addressing Parsees he said :—

"I am to prove to you that your faith rests upon the rock of truth, the living rock of Occult Science." (p. 139). "No religion has profounder truths, deeper spiritual truths, concealed under its familiar mask. than yours." p. 157.

"I, a Western man, taught in a Western University, and nursed on the traditions of modern civilization, say that Zaratushta knew more about nature than Tyndall does, more about the laws of force than Balfour Stewart, more about the origin of species than Darwin or Hæckel, more about the human mind and its potentialities than Maudsley or Bain. And so did Buddha and some other proficients in Occult Science." p. 149.

Mr. Judge, addressing some Madras students, bore the following testimony to Hindu Philosophy :—

"The great Indian nation produced its Sanskrit. Great consideration was due to this language. It contained Philosophy as refined as Herbert Spencer's, and further it used language that Herbert Spencer could not understand. His very ideas were to be found in Indian philosophy elaborated to such an extent that Spencer would do well to throw his books into the sea and apply himself to the study of Hindu Philosophy." *Madras Mail*, Sept. 29, 1884.

Mrs. Besant seems to be pursuing the same course.

The Indian Social Reformer, one of the best Native papers in India, expects the following from her:

"Mrs. BESANT is coming; her oratory will make her the idol of the hour. The Hindu will get his ancestors praised to the skies.

"We are sure there will be much outward sympathy; our countrymen will be mightily pleased with Mrs. Besant, because all that she may say will tickle their vanity." Nov. 25, 1893.

Intelligent Indians dislike such flattery, *especially from charlatans who flatter with a purpose.*

Dr. Bhandarkar, late Professor of Sanskrit, Deccan College, Poona, is probably the most eminent Indian scholar of the present time. What is his advice to his countrymen?

"Here I feel myself in duty bound even at the risk of displeasing some of you, to make passing allusion to the most uncritical spirit that has come over us of praising ourselves and our ancestors indiscriminately, seeing nothing but good in our institutions and in our ancient literature, asserting that the ancient Hindus had made very great progress in all the sciences, physical, moral, and social, and the arts,—greater even by far than Europe has made hitherto—and denying even the most obvious deficiencies in our literature, such as the absence of satisfactory historical records, and our most obvious defects. As long as this spirit exists in us, we can never hope to throw light on our ancient history, and on the excellencies and defects of our race, and never hope to rise."

Bengalis are peculiarly prone to indulge in vain boastings regarding the ancient civilization of India. Mr. Manomohun Ghose remarked some time ago in Calcutta:

"He felt a legitimate pride in the ancient civilization of India, but he was bound to say that an undue and exaggerated veneration for the past was doing a great deal of mischief. It was quite sickening to hear the remark made at almost every public meeting that the ancient civilization of India was superior far to that which Europe ever had." ...

"It must be admitted by all who have carefully studied the ancient literature of India that the much-vaunted civilization of India was of a peculiar type, and that it never could bear any comparison to what we call modern European civilization. Whatever might be the case in ancient times, he thought that this frequent appeal to our ancient civilization could serve no good purpose at the present day, while it was simply calculated to make the Bengalis more conceited than they were."

To the above testimonies from Bombay and Bengal, may be added the opinion of an Indian Professor in the Presidency College, Madras:—

"We take this opportunity of protesting against the appeal to false patriotism which Mrs. Besant is making in every one of her lectures. We believe she has learnt this trick from Col. Olcott. Nothing has been a cause of such incalculable harm to the cause of progress and truth in this country as the flattering of the vanity of Indians by referring in season and out of season to the greatness of their ancestors. Whenever an allusion is made to their ancient and learned forefathers, the great truths embodied in their ancient Hindu Scriptures, the grand lessons which the West has to learn from the East, &c., our countrymen are flattered immensely, but such talk only helps to keep them in a fool's paradise. It renders them proud and indolent, and makes them oppose blindly every effort made to raise them from the deplorable condition in which they are at present. We have no doubt that Theosophy will be the rage with our countrymen for some months more, but the really thinking portion of the educated community will know what value to attach to this temporary outburst of enthusiasm in favour of the creed of Blavatsky and Olcott."

Macaulay says in his famous "Minute" on Education in India, that the civilization of Russia was effected,

"Not by flattering national prejudices; not by feeding the mind of the young Muscovite with the old woman's stories which his rude forefathers had believed .... not by calling him 'a learned native,' when he has mastered all these points of knowledge; but by teaching him those foreign languages in which the greatest mass of information had been laid up, and thus putting all taht information within his reach. The languages of Western Europe civilized Russia, I cannot doubt that they will do for the Hindu what they have done for the Tartar."

Mrs. Besant is said to have "been immensely pleased with the reception being accorded to her in Southern India." This is not surprising, since she has declared herself a Hindu.

The Tinnevelly correspondent of the *Madras Standard* thus explains why Mrs. Besant had a crowded audience in that town :—

"The rumour that a learned gentleman and a wonderful lady who have mastered the Hindu religious books and literature were going to explain the mysteries of the ancient Vedas, and to prove the unrivalled excellence of the Hindu religion had spread like wild fire. Hundreds of people who did not know one word of the English language were pressing and crushing one another, at least to see them, and to hear them pronounce the sacred words 'Sri Krishna' and 'Arjuna.' There is great virtue in hearing the name of a god pronounced by a European." November 27, 1893.

When the "Hierophant" and his "venerated female companion," professed Buddhism in Ceylon, they had "almost a royal progress," through the Buddhist districts of the Island. Longer experience has taught Colonel Olcott and Mr. Edge to rate such receptions at their proper value. "We feel honoured when we are decked with wreaths and garlands, it is pleasant to hear one's praises sung, no doubt, but—we are not deluded." (See page 64).

MRS. BESANT'S "LOYALTY TO TRUTH."

Mrs. Besant's Guru, as already quoted, professed the highest admiration of *truth*. The motto of *The Theosophist* is, "There is no Religion higher than Truth;" The "moral standard of *The Theosophist* is TRUTH;" a Theosophist banner had the inscription, "There is no Duty higher than Truth." That noble virtue deserves to be held in the highest esteem. There are, however, some Indians who consider it *patriotic* to lie for the credit of their country, to defend superstitions and customs which their consciences condemn. The late Sir Madava Row lays down the right course :

"**What is NOT TRUE, is NOT PATRIOTIC**."

This should be indelibly impressed on the minds of educated Indians.

The Chela does not fall below her Guru in her professed admiration of truth. In *Why I became a Theosopher*, Mrs. Besant claims loyalty to truth as the distinguishing feature of her character. She asks for no other epitaph on her tomb, but

"SHE TRIED TO FOLLOW TRUTH."

It is very remarkable that she should have chosen as her *Guru* a consummate hypocrite, who was "*consciously weaving an enormous net-work of falsehood in all her writings, acts and conversation for the last eight or nine years.*"

It is granted that until Mrs. Besant made the acquaintance of Madame Blavatsky she may claim to have acted up, in some measure, to her chosen epitaph, however much her search may have been misdirected. The sacrifices which she made are proof of this. Of late years, however, she has passed from extreme scepticism to "voracious credulity." Mr. Stead describes her as "sitting at the feet of Madame Blavatsky, and learning like a little child all the lore of the Mahatmas." She seems now almost incapable of distinguishing between truth and falsehood.

Borderland, for October, 1893, contains Mrs. Besant's "Story of her Conversion" to Theosophy. The following extract describes the turning point:

"The Charges against H. P. B.

"And so it came to pass that I went again to Lansdowne-road to ask about the Theosophical Society. H. P. Blavatsky looked at me piercingly for a moment: 'Have you read the report about me of the Society for Psychical Research?' 'No, I never heard of it so far as I know.' 'Go and read it, and if, after reading it, you come back—well.' And nothing more would she say on the subject, but branched off to her experiences in many lands.

"I borrowed a copy of the report, read and re-read it. Quickly I saw how slender was the foundation on which the imposing structure was built. The continual assumptions on which conclusions were based; the incredible character of the allegations; the most damning fact of all—the foul source from which the evidence was derived. Everything turned on the veracity of the Coulombs, and they were self-stamped as partners in the alleged frauds. Could I put such against the frank fearless nature that I had caught a glimpse of, against the proud fiery truthfulness that shone at me from the clear blue eyes— honest and fearless as those of a noble child? Was the writer of 'The Secret Doctrine,' at this miserable impostor, this accomplice of tricksters, this foul and loathsome deceiver, this conjurer with trap-doors and sliding panels? I laughed aloud at the absurdity, and flung the report aside with the righteous scorn of an honest nature that knew its own kin when it met them, and shrank from the foulness and baseness of a lie. The next day saw me at the Theosophical Publishing Company's Office at 7, Duke-Street, Adelphi, where Countess Wachtmeister,—one of the leafest of H. P. B's friends—was at work, and I signed an application to be admitted as Fellow of the Theosophical Society." p. 175.

Mrs. Besant, like Mr. Sinnett, sees the gravity of the situation. Mr. Sinnett admits that either Madame Blavatsky's "*statements concerning the Brothers are broadly true or she has consciously been weaving an enormous net-work of falsehood in all her writings, acts, and conversation for the last eight or nine years.*"* Mrs. Besant makes the alternative even stronger: Madame Blavatsky has been a *miserable impostor, the accomplice of tricksters, the foul and loathsome deceiver, the conjurer with trap doors and sliding panels.*"

One would have thought that such a serious alternative would have been long and carefully investigated. Like a woman, Mrs. Besant soon jumped at a foregone conclusion. Within twenty-four hours she discovered that the charges were baseless, and had become a member of the Society.

What was it that made the Report of Professor Sidgwick and Mr. Hodgson's Account of Personal Investigation in India to have no more weight than the small dust of the balance?

"*The proud fiery truthfulness that shone at me from the clear blue eyes—honest and fearless as those of a noble child.*"

Mrs. Besant's chief reason for arriving at her conclusion seems to have been the "foul source," from which the charges emanated—"the Coulombs, self-stamped as partners in the alleged frauds." She fails to see that this is a strong presumption against Madame Blavatsky. The latter made Mrs. Coulomb's acquaintance in Egypt when she was engaged in a "materialization show business."† When she started afresh in the same line, she invited both to India. M. Coulomb was a skilful mechanic, able to construct shrines with sliding panels; Madame Coulomb was an adept in preparing masks and the other paraphernalia required for the "phenomena." Correspondence shows that Madame Blavatsky and Madame Coulomb were associated together for years on the most familiar terms. Mrs. Coulomb, "the foul source," was addressed as " My

---

* *The Occult World*, pp. 152, 153.
† See page 23. *Madame Blavatsky, her Tricks, and her Dupes*, now in preparation, will give details about the " phenomena."

dear Marquise." More than this. In a letter from Colombo, dated June 16, 1880, Madame Blavatsky writes:

"My dear Mme. Coulomb,
"You are one of my 'Assistant Secretaries" (See Rules); you are my friend—and that is more."
"Yours in the love of Buddha,
H. P. B.*"

"Birds of a feather flock together." The characters of the two must have had something in common. Another proverb says, "When rogues fall out, their knaveries come to light." The trickery was discovered when the Coulombs were turned out of the Theosophist quarters at Madras.

Mrs. Besant read the Report of the Psychical Research Society so perfunctorily, that she says, "*every thing turned on the veracity of the Coulomb.*" She is totally mistaken. The Report shows plainly (see page 17), that due caution was exercised in this point. The trickery was established by *seventy or eighty of Madame Blavatsky's own letters*. It is alleged that they were forged by Madame Coulomb. The *Madras Christian College Magazine* thus replies to this charge:—

"The letters in our possession are all marked with the impress of a single character,—that of a woman, clever, witty and passionate; ready of speech and fertile in resource; now full of kindness, now of fury and contempt. . . To have drawn a character like the Madame Blavatsky of our letters, so full of daring contradictions, yet possessed of such breathing life and consistency, would be a literary achievement worthy of our greatest dramatist." Vol. II. pp. 305, 306.

To forge even a signature is not easy; to forge seventy or eighty letters of the above description is impossible. In addition, experts in London have declared them to be genuine.

The Case for Decision.—Mrs. Besant *versus* the following:
1. The careful inquiry of the Editor of the *Madras Christian College Magazine*, with whom undoubtedly agreed Dr. Miller and the other College Professors. Madame Blavatsky was publicly challenged to prove that

---
* *Christian College Magazine*, Vol. II, pp. 292, 293.

the letters were forgeries. The Editor incurred the risk of very heavy damages if she had gained her case.

2. The minute examination of Mr. R Hodgson, a Cambridge graduate, who spent three months in India carefully sifting the alleged "phenomena."

3. The evidence of the man whom India now "delights to honour"—MR. A. O. HUME—the Father of the National Congress.

At first Mr. Hume was taken with Madame Blavatsky. She lived in his family for some time. One of the alleged "phenomena" was the recovery of Mrs. Hume's brooch.

Mr. Hume bears testimony to the frequent inaccuracy of Madame Blavatsky's statements:

"Madame Blavatsky's converse is ... too often replete with contradictions, inaccuracies, and at times apparently distinct misstatements."*

He was disgusted also with the "hatred, malice, and all uncharitableness," exhibited by the "Founders," notwithstanding the profession of a "religion of tolerance, charity, kindness," (See pages 53, 54).

Mr. Hodgson says in his Report:

"I enjoyed, while in India, the opportunity of having various long interviews with Mr. Hume, and have already referred to his conclusion (reached after a most careful inquiry) in connection with the incident of the recovery of Mrs. Hume's brooch, that Madame Blavatsky may very well have obtained the brooch previously by ordinary methods. Long before the publication of the Blavatsky-Coulomb letters in the *Christian College Magazine*, Mr. Hume had discovered that some of Madame Blavatsky's phenomena were fraudulent, and that some of the professed Mahatma writing was the handiwork of Madame Blavatsky herself. Once or twice he had seen notes on some philosophic questions which had been made by Mr. Subba Row (Vakil of the High Court, Madras), a leading native Theosophist, the substance of these notes appeared afterwards worked up into a Mahatma document (received by either himself or Mr. Sinnett) and worsened in the working."†

Mr. Coleman says that *Esoteric Buddhism* "was originally to be written by Mr. Hume, and he commenced to

---

* *Hints on Esoteric Philosophy*, No. 1. p. 68.
† Proceedings of the Psychical Research Society, Dec. 1885, p. 274.

prepare it for the press; but he got disgusted with the contradictions, inconsistencies, falsehoods, and double-dealing manifested by the adepts in their correspondence with him, and he accordingly severed all connection with them and with Madame Blavatsky." (See page 27.)

4. The Report of the Committee of the Psychical Research Society, written by Professor Sidgwick, after the receipt of Mr. Hodgson's Account of his Investigations and the examination of a number of Madame Blavatsky's letters, in which she is characterised as an "impostor."

In opposition to such a conclusive body of evidence, most of it from India, and when the alleged "phenomena" were quite recent, we have the mere assertion of Mrs. Besant, seven years later, after twenty-four hours study, and without seeing a single original letter on which the charges were founded.

There is a superabundance of lawyers in India. Would any of them (without fee!) prepare a *Brief* on the case: Mrs. Besant *versus* the *Madras Christian College Magazine* and others?

Explanation of Mrs. Besant's Attitude.—Two reasons may be given :—

1. *Her pride of intellect.*—The saying of Plato has been quoted, that "Atheism is a disease of the soul before it becomes an error of the understanding." Mrs. Besant, referring to a former Freethinking fellow-labourer says :—

"Mr. Foote writes with exceeding bitterness that amidst all her changes Mrs. Besant remains quite positive."*

Her astute Guru saw through her character. "Child," she said to me long afterwards, "your pride is terrible; you are as proud as Lucifer himself."†

Many good men have passed through a "horror of great darkness," caused by sceptical doubts, like those described by Sir William Muir (See page 98). The late Dr. Arnold is a well-known example.

Sir William Muir points out the means to be employed

---

* *Why I became a Theosophist*, p. 6.
† *Borderland*, Oct. 1893, p. 175.

and their happy issue. Mrs. Besant proudly trusted to her own intellect. Instead of humbly asking light from above, she impiously challenged the Almighty to do His worst. (See page 69).

2. *Hypnotic influence.*—Madame Blavatsky claims to have reduced Colonel Olcott to the condition of a "psychologised baby," "so that he did not know his head from his heels."

The *New York Herald,* in reviewing Mr. Sinnett's *Occult World,* gives the similar explanation, so far as he is concerned:—

"To psychologists the book will be interesting as a study of a feeble mind subordinated to a stronger intelligence, and under that influence accepting as facts things as ridiculous as ever were believed by a person mesmerized. Mr. Sinnett's belief in the occult manifestations fed to him at Madame Blavatsky's sweet will, as green food is doled out to a donkey, is wonderfully amusing. All the flummery about the brotherhood in the mountains of Thibet, the difficulty of getting near them in the flesh, their psychic telephone and so on, is swallowed with avidity."

Like Mr. Sinnett, Mrs. Besant professes her belief in the reality of the *phenomena,* and to have *seen* a Mahatma. (See page 70).

The Report of the British Medical Association, quoted in *Borderland,* says:—

"Among the mental phenomena of hypnotism are altered consciousness, temporary limitation of will pour, increased receptivity of suggestion from without, sometimes to the extent of producing passing delusions, illusions, and hallucinations, an exalted condition of the attention, and post-hypnotic suggestions." Oct. 1893. p. 186.

The above is the most charitable explanation of Mrs. Besant's conduct.

DUTY OF MRS. BESANT.

Mrs. Besant's outrageous flattery of the Hindus is scarcely consistent with her zeal for truth. Although eagerly swallowed by the ignorant and half-educated, thoughtful intelligent men deprecate it from its injurious effects. As already mentioned, she uses it because she has "an axe to grind."

Instead of going about lecturing on "phenomena" which were proved to be frauds years ago, or on Mahatmas proved to be charlatans, plagiarists and liars, let her examine carefully the charges brought against Madame Blavatsky, and the documents on which they are based.

Mr. W. Emmette Coleman, of the Chief Quartermaster's Office, San Francisco, California, has collected a very large number of Madame Blavatsky's letters and those professed to have come from Mahatmas. Among others, Mr. Hume gave the letters which he had received. Mr. Coleman says:—

"Mr. Hume in a letter in 1883 to Madame Blavatsky, the original of which is in my possession, told her that he knew that she wrote all the Morya letters and some at least of those signed K. H." See page 30.

Mr. Coleman can also show Mrs. Besant the sources from which *Isis Unveiled*, *The Secret Doctrine*, the bogus *Book of Dzyan*, &c. were plagiarised.

If Mrs. Besant, instead of following the above course, persists in going about lecturing on Manu's Code, phenomena, Mahatmas, re-incarnation, &c., she will prove that her zeal for the truth is much on a par with that of her Guru.

Mrs. Besant's Gospel.

For ten years or more Mrs. Besant, both by her voice and her pen, advocated the most ruinous errors of atheism and materialism. She might well be compared to a "madman who casteth fire-brands, arrows, and death." How many souls have thus been destroyed by her, it is impossible to tell. It is true that she now acknowledges materialism to be wrong, and preaches re-incarnation; but her Gospel to a "sin-burdened world" is the same as that of Colonel Olcott:—

"Eternal, immutable law punishes the slightest moral sins as certainly as it does every physical sin; and, that as man creates his own destiny, so *he* must be his own Saviour and Redeemer, and can have no other." *Addresses*, p. 38.

Mr. Stead has the following remarks on this message:—

"There is no note which vibrates more constantly in the soul of every true man—and the truer he is the more it vibrates—than the prayer of the publican; 'God be merciful to me, a sinner!' That despairing cry rises from the deepest and innermost recesses of our being. It finds an answer in the story of the woman taken in adultery, in the parable of the Prodigal, in the death of the Crucified. To that heart-felt cry I do not find an answer in Theosophy. I find, on the contrary, an almost exultant assertion of the opposing doctrines, that God is not a Being with a father's heart, that for sin there is no expiation, and for the sinner no pardon." *Review of Reviews*, Vol. IV. p. 367.

The subject of Mrs. Besant's first lecture in Madras is THE DANGERS OF MATERIALISM. This undoubtedly is the greatest bane of educated Hindus. Although there is a small band of earnest reformers among them, many have embraced what is appropriately called the "pig philosophy." "Let us eat and drink for to-morrow we die." They may be zealous for political reform, as it holds out the hope of a larger share of the official "loaves and fishes;" but to social and moral reform, they are perfectly indifferent. The Madras Social Reform Society numbers less than 50 members, and had to apply to a European to preside at its first anniversary. Men of the above class seek only the pleasures of the world. At times they may be startled by the sudden death of one of their number; but they speedily relapse into their state of apathy, without regard to the eternity to which they are speeding, and into which they may enter at any moment.

This state of things applies not simply to Madras, but to many of the large cities of India.

Though several causes have contributed to it, perhaps the principal has been the circulation of "free thought" literature. Mrs. Besant's, *My Path to Atheism*, Mr. Bradlaugh's, *Is there a God? Has Man a Soul?* Ingersoll's writings, &c. have done incalculable mischief.

Mrs. Besant lectures eloquently on the dangers of the materialism; but she omits the strongest argument against it—the belief in an intelligent Creator and Governor of the

Universe. She will also find it a much harder task to uproot error than to sow it.

Mrs. Besant now denounces the doctrine which she once zealously advocated. This might well make her hesitate in trying to teach the Hindus that "God is not a Being with a father's heart, that for sin there is no expiation, and for the sinner no pardon." A terrible responsibility will rest upon her if she does so. Her eloquence will draw vast crowds of educated Hindus, and her skill will help her to "make the worse appear the better cause"; but persisting in her course, she will be like the fabled Sirens who by their melodious voices lured mariners to their destruction.

The "WISDOM RELIGION" has taught Colonel Olcott that "the idea of a personal God is only a gigantic shadow thrown upon the void of space by the imagination of ignorant men." Mrs. Besant presents the same combination of scepticism and "voracious credulity." She rejects the "concept of a personal God as impossible," although it has been held by the wisest and best men in all ages; she accepts as truth the statements of a convicted trickster and liar, although condemned as "rubbish" by men like Max Müller and Monier Williams.

The many phases of belief and unbelief through which Mrs. Besant has passed, show that she is a most unsafe religious guide. Mr. Stead thinks that her changes have not yet terminated: "The prediction made long ago that Mrs. Besant would die in the odour of sanctity within the pale of the Catholic Church seems to be progressing towards its fulfilment."*

Concluding Remarks.

Colonel Olcott's experience does not lead one to hope that any great results will follow from the foregoing exposure. As already quoted (page 11), he says that "Mediums caught red-handed in trickery, are able to make their dupes regard them as martyrs, and the damning

---

* *Review of Reviews*, August 1891, p. 143.

proofs of their guilt, as having been secretly supplied by the unbelievers themselves to strike a blow at their holy cause." Still, it is hoped that some good will be done.

Professor Max Müller condemns Madame Blavatsky's works as full of errors (See page 4). In the Appendix (Page 102) educated Hindus are recommended to study their own religion through its recognised standards. Should the visit of Mrs. Besant lead to greater religious inquiry, it will not have been altogether an evil.

The gross frauds of Madame Blavatsky and the great ignorance both of her and Mrs. Besant have been freely exposed to prevent the millions of India from being led away by pernicious error. While this has been done as a bounden duty, may that great Being whose existence Mrs. Besant denied, and would place man upon "His usurped throne," have mercy on His erring child! May her great powers yet be employed to diffuse the faith which she has so long sought to destroy!

10. GOD OUR HEAVENLY FATHER.

It is generally admitted that Hinduism has become more and more impure as centuries have rolled on. At present it is commonly said that there are 33 crores of divinities. Some Hindus, unacquainted with the Vedas, think that they contain a pure monotheism. Such is not the case. The religion of the Vedas is polytheistic. The gods are usually spoken of as thrice-eleven, with their wives, as the following quotations will show:

In the third Mandala of the Rig-Veda, Hymn 6, verse 10, Agni is thus addressed:

"Bring, with their wives, the gods, the three-and-thirty, after thy god-like nature, and be joyful."

The following invitation is given to the Asvins:—

"Come O Nasatyas, with the thrice eleven gods; come, O ye Asvins to the drinking of the meath." I. 34. 11.

A hymn to the Visvedevas concludes thus:

"O ye eleven gods whose home is heaven, O ye eleven who make earth your dwelling,
Ye who with might, eleven, live in waters, accept this sacrifice,
O gods, with pleasure." I. 139. 11.*

It will be seen that the gods are reduced in number from 33 crores to 33 with their wives. In Book iv. 9. 9. the gods are mentioned as being much more numerous: "Three hundred, three thousand, thirty and nine gods have worshipped Agni."

Many Hindus suppose that monotheism is taught in the well-known formula from the Chhandogya Upanishad, *ekam evadvitiyam*, "One only without a second." This is a mistake. The real meaning is, not that there is only one God, but that there is no second anything—a totally different doctrine.

But let us go back beyond the Vedas to the time when the Eastern and Western Aryans lived together somewhere in Central Asia, and we find monotheism.

The Oldest Aryan Religion.—This may best be explained in the words of Max Müller:—

"Thousands of years ago, before Greek was Greek, and Sanskrit was Sanskrit, the ancestors of the Aryan races dwelt together in the high lands of Central Asia, speaking one common language.

"The terms for God, for house, for father, mother, son and daughter, for dog and cow, for heart and tears, for axe and tree, identical in all the Indo-European idioms are like the watchwords of soldiers. We challenge the seeming stranger; and whether he answer with the lips of a Greek, a German, or an Indian, we recognise him as one of ourselves. There *was* a time when the ancestors of the Celts, the Germans, the Slavonians, the Greeks and Italians, the Persians and Hindus, were living together within the same fences, separate from the ancestors of the Semitic and Turanian races."

---

* See *An Account of the Vedas*, with translations of some of the most important hymns. 8vo. 165 pp. Sold by Mr. A. T. Scott, Tract Depôt, Madras. Price 4¼ As.; with postage, 6 As.

"The Aryans were then no longer dwellers in tents, but builders of permanent houses. As the name for king is the same in Sanskrit, Latin, Teutonic, and Celtic, we know that kingly government was established and recognised by the Aryans at the prehistoric period. They also worshipped an unseen Being, under the self-same name."*

"If I were asked what I consider the most important discovery which has been made during the nineteenth century with respect to the ancient history of mankind, I should answer by the following short line:

Sanskrit DYAUSH-PITAR = Greek ΖΕΤΣΠΑΤΗΡ (ZEUS PATER)=Latin JUPITER=Old Norse TYR.

"Think what this equation implies! It implies not only that our own ancestors and the ancestors of Homer and Cicero (the Greeks and Romans) spoke the same language as the people of India—this is a discovery which, however incredible it sounded at first, has long ceased to cause any surprise—but it implies and proves that they all had once the same faith, and worshipped for a time the same supreme Deity under exactly the same name—a name which meant Heaven-Father.

"If we wish to realise to its fullest extent the unbroken continuity in the language, in the thoughts and words of the principal Aryan nations, let us look at the accents in the following list:—†

	Sanskrit.	Greek.
Nom.	Dyaús.	Ζεύς
Gen.	Divás.	Διός
Loc.	Diví.	Διΐ
Acc.	Dívam.	Δία
Voc.	Dyaŭs.	Ζεῦ

"Here we see that at the time when the Greeks had become such thorough Greeks that they hardly knew of the existence of India, the people at Athens laid the accent in the oblique cases of Zeus on exactly the same syllable on which the Brahmans laid it at Benares, with this dif-

---
* *Ancient Sanskrit Literature.*
† *Nineteenth Century*, Oct: 1885. pp. 626, 627.

ference only, that the Brahmans knew the reason why, while the Athenians did not."

"There is a monotheism which precedes the polytheism of the Veda, and even in the invocation of their innumerable gods, the remembrance of a God, one and infinite, breaks through the mist of an idolatrous phraseology, like the blue sky that is hidden by passing clouds."

"Thousands of years have passed away since the Aryan nations separated to travel to the North and the South, the West and the East: they have each formed their languages, they have each founded empires and philosophies, they have each built temples and razed them to the ground; they have all grown older, and it may be wiser and better; but when they search for a name for that which is most exalted and yet most dear to every one of us, when they wish to express both awe and love, the infinite and the finite, they can but do what their old fathers did when gazing up the eternal sky, and feeling the presence of a Being as far as far and as near as near can be; they can but combine the self-same words and utter once more the primeval Aryan prayer, Heaven Father, in that form which will endure for ever, "Our Father, which art in heaven."*

Educated Hindus! go back to the monotheism which Max Müller says "precedes the polytheism of the Veda." Return to the worship of our great Father in heaven.

God is our father by creation. To Him we owe our existence. We are dependent upon Him for every breath we draw; we live upon His earth; it is His sun that shines upon us. Every thing we have belongs to Him.

What is the duty of a child to a father? He should love him; he should delight in his presence, he should often speak to him; he should obey him cheerfully, honour him, and seek in all things to please him.

Have we treated our heavenly Father in this way? Alas, no! We have been disobedient, ungrateful children, often refusing to obey Him, giving the honour due to Him to the

---

* *Science of Religion*, pp. 172, 173.

works of our own hands or living in utter forgetfulness of Him.

Still, God regards us with a father's love. His message to us is, "Return, ye backsliding children, and I will heal your backslidings." This is beautifully taught by Jesus Christ in the parable of the Prodigal Son.

A son asked from his father the portion of goods that fell to him. As soon as he had received it, he went to a far country, where he soon spent all that he had among wicked companions. He was so poor that he was sent to take care of swine, and so hungry that he would gladly have filled his belly with some of the food that the swine did eat.

Afterwards he thought that while he was starving, his father's servants had enough and to spare. Then he said to himself, "I will arise and go to my father, and will say to him, Father I have sinned against heaven and in thy sight, and am no more worthy to be called thy son." As soon as his father saw him coming, he ran, fell on his neck and kissed him. Then the father said to his servants, "Bring forth the best robe and put it on him; and put a ring on his hand, and shoes on his feet." He also ordered them to make ready the daintiest food. Full of joy he said, "This my son was dead and is alive again; he was lost and is found." Luke xv.

This parable is a faint emblem of God's willingness to receive repenting sinners.

But God is more than our Father; He is also our King. Satisfaction is needed for His broken law. Even Hinduism recognises the idea of God becoming incarnate to lighten the burden of pain and misery under which the universe is groaning. What is thus shadowed forth, is clearly revealed in the Christian scriptures.

God's message to a "sin-burdened world," is not that of Buddha or Theosophy. Knowing our need of Divine help, He has sent from heaven One "mighty to save." When the Lord Jesus Christ was on earth, He gave the gracious invitation: "Come unto me all ye that labour and are heavy laden, and I will give you rest."

Though the reader may be able only to

"Stretch the lame hands of faith and grope,"

let him go to the Saviour, asking the fulfilment of this promise.

Space does not permit the way of salvation to be fully explained. The reader is referred to *Short Papers for Seekers after Truth,* or to Dr. Murray Mitchell's *Elements of Christian Truth,* containing lectures to educated Hindus. But, above all, the *New Testament*[*] should be studied. A commencement may be made with the Gospel of Luke, originally written for a heathen convert, as it contains some explanations not necessary for Jewish readers.

Sir William Muir, formerly Lieut.-Governor of the North-West Provinces, and now Principal of the University of Edinburgh, gave the following advice to Calcutta students who were seeking after truth :—

"I am well aware that in the search you will probably have to pass through a land of doubt and darkness. The ancient land-marks to which you have been used to look up as the beacons that would guide you all your life through, may perhaps vanish from your sight, and you well be left to grope for your way in perplexity and doubt; and yet, I can only wish for all of you that you may enter into it, if haply thereby you may emerge into a better light than you now possess.

"To any who may endure this experience, and find themselves enveloped in thick darkness, not knowing where to turn, I would offer two admonitions by way of caution.

"However dark and confused the elements may be about you, hold firmly by those grand principles of morality and virtue which are inculcated upon you here. Under the pretext of liberty, of advanced thought, and of an enlightened faith, the temptation will come to you of latitudinarian Ethics and a lax code of Morals. Reject the temptation; it is but a meretricious blandishment, a Siren smile alluring you to ruin. Reject every proposal that would confound

---

[*] Copies may be obtained at the Bible Depôts scattered over India.
Scriptures are sold at the Bible Depôt, Memorial Hall, Madras, at the following rates :—
Ruby New Testament, 24mo. (Small type) 1 An. with postage 1½ As.
Minion   Do.   24mo. (Larger type) 3 As.   „   4½ As.
Ruby Bible,   16mo.   Sheep   4 As.   „   6½ As.
Nonpareil Bible, 16mo. Basil; with Maps and Reference, 8 As. 11 As.
The last is specially recommended.

the eternal obligations of Right and Wrong, of Virtue and Vice: use hardness as good soldiers: practise self-denial. And thus, however dark the night, you will at least be saved from sinking in the quagmire of materialism and sensuality.

"But this is not enough. A higher help is needed; and in your darkest hour a Friend is near at hand ready to help.

"I remember a very good and very learned man telling me that, in a season of illness, the idea of the existence of all created things passed away from him: his mind became a blank; there was nothing he could lay hold of. Yes, there was one idea left; it was that of his Maker as his Father. To this he clung, and his poor dark mind had peace and rest.

"And so do you, my dear young friends. If you enter a land of doubt and thick darkness,—the very ground sinking beneath your feet; the staff on which you had leant and hoped to lean safely all your life, crumbling in your hand,—remember that He, your God and Father, is near to you; not impassive or unmindful of you; but ready to afford you aid, if you will duly seek it. He has told us that He is 'nigh unto all them that call upon Him, to all that call upon Him in truth.' Remember this condition, it must be '*in truth*' that you seek His aid, with the earnest and sincere resolve to follow His guidance whithersoever it will lead you.

"When you walk in darkness, and there is no light, make Him your refuge. Thus will light spring up. Peace will return. You will again walk on sure and firm ground— aye, far surer and firmer than any ground you ever trod upon before."

Repentant children are drawn far more closely to God than those who are merely His children by creation, and are still living in disobedience. They will have a father's *eye* to watch over them. Wherever they are, by day or by night, they can never be out of His sight. They will have the *ear* of a father to listen to their requests. They will have a father's *hand* to guide and protect them. They will have a father's *home* to receive them at last, there to dwell with Him for ever.

O the happiness of having God for a Father! The greatest king could not do for you what God can; His wealth can never fail; His power can never become weak; His love knows no decay. "Alone we entered the world, alone we depart." But if God is our Father, we can confidently say, "Yea, though I walk through the valley of the shadow of death, I will fear no evil; for Thou art with me."

Let no tongue, however persuasive, rob you of the great truth of the FATHERHOOD OF GOD, and its corollary, the BROTHERHOOD OF MAN.

The following short prayers for light may be fitly offered:

Show me Thy ways, O Lord; teach me Thy paths; Lead me in Thy truth and teach me; for Thou art the God of my salvation.

Cause me to know the way wherein I should walk; for I lift my soul to Thee.

O all-wise, all-merciful God and Father, pour the bright beams of Thy light into my soul, and guide me into Thy eternal truth.

The following prayer for spiritual light is attributed to Augustine, one of the most distinguished early Christians, born in Africa, 354 A.D.

O Lord, who art the Light, the Way, the Truth, the Life; in whom there is no darkness, error, vanity, nor death; the light, without which there is darkness; the way, without which there is wandering; the truth, without which there is error; the life, without which there is death; say, Lord, 'Let there be light,' and I shall see light and eschew darkness; I shall see the way, and avoid wandering; I shall see the truth, and shun error; I shall see life and escape death. Illuminate, O illuminate my blind soul, which sitteth in darkness and the shadow of death; and direct my feet in the way of peace.

If we make use of the light we possess, more will be given; if we act contrary to it, the light is gradually extinguished.

A man who indulges in vice of any kind cannot expect to arrive at the truth. Of the successful searcher Tennyson says:

"Perplext in faith, but pure in deeds,
At last he beats his music out."

The following prayer which Jesus Christ taught His disciples may be used daily:

"Our Father which art in heaven, Hallowed be Thy name. Thy Kingdom come. Thy will be done in earth as it is in heaven. Give us this day our daily bread. And forgive us our debts as we forgive our debtors. And lead us not into temptation, but deliver us from evil. For Thine is the kingdom, and the power, and the glory, for ever. Amen.

It has been shown that there was a time when the ancestors of the Hindus, Persians, English, French, Germans, and others, were living together in Central Asia, worshipping the same God under the self-same name—Heaven Father May the time soon come when both Eastern and Western Aryans will kneel at the same throne of grace, and offer the same grand old prayer!

FATHER, LEAD ON!

My Father God, lead on!
Calmly I follow where Thy guiding hand
Directs my steps. I would not trembling stand,
 Though all before the way
 Is dark as night. I stay
 My soul on Thee, and say :
Father, I trust Thy love; lead on.

Thou givest strength: lead on!
I cannot sink while Thy right hand upholds,
Nor comfort lack while Thy kind arm enfolds.
 Through all my soul I feel
 A healing influence steal,
 While at thy feet I kneel,
Father, in lowly trust: lead on.

'T will soon be o'er; lead on!
Left all behind, earth's heart-aches then shall seem
E'en as the memories of a vanished dream;
 And when of griefs and tears
 The golden fruit appears,
 Around the eternal years,
Father, all thanks be Thine! Lead on!

RAY PALMER.

APPENDIX.

CATALOGUE OF ENGLISH PUBLICATIONS

FOR

INDIAN READERS.

INTRODUCTORY REMARKS ON THE STUDY OF HINDUISM.

While books full of error, like those of Madame Blavatsky, are worse than useless, educated Hindus are recommended to study their own religion through its recognised standards. A beginning should be made with the Vedas, on which it is professedly based. Formerly their contents were almost unknown; copies of the Rig-Veda, the most important, are now easily procurable.

Sanskrit Text of the Rig-Vēda.

The Text, with Sayana's Commentary, edited by Professor Max Müller is sold in 4 volumes, price £8-8-0.

The Text alone, edited by Professor Peterson, is included in the Bombay Sanskrit Series.

Translations.

Only a very few Indian scholars are able to understand the Rig-Veda in Sanskrit : an imperfect knowledge of the language is worthless for this purpose. English translations, however, by competent scholars give a fair idea of the original.

There is a translation of the whole work by Professor Wilson and others; Professor Max Müller has one in progress. The best and cheapest complete translation now available is by Mr. R. T. GRIFFITH, for many years Principal of the Government College, Benares, where he had the assistance of the ablest pandits in India. Valuable explanatory notes are added throughout. It is published by E. J. Lazarus & Co., Benares, Price Rs. 16 in 16 parts; or Rs. 19-12-0 in 4 volumes.

If possible, the complete translation should be obtained; but as this is beyond the means of most, the cheap selection mentioned in the note on page 94 may be used. With the kind permission of Mr. Griffith, it contains a few of the most important hymns, in whole or in part, from the ten Mandalas. The first hymn is given in Nagri and Roman character as well as in English. The hymns quoted in full include one addressed by Sunahsepa to Varuna when bound to the sacrificial post, and the celebrated Purusha Sukta hymn.

There are selections from 11 hymns in the Atharva Veda. One of them is regarded as a spell, "To recall from Death." Short extracts from the Aitareya Brahmana and the Satapatha Brahmana give some idea of their character.

There is an Introduction of 66 pages, compiled from the works of Max Müller, Muir, Haug, Whitney, Rajendra Lala Mitra, and others, which will be found very useful.

Scattered over India there are Hindu Literary Societies. A course of study of the Rig-Veda would be interesting and instructive.

Hindu Philosophy.

This is a large and difficult subject. Translations of the twelve principal Upanishads can be obtained in Bombay. Those edited by Max Müller are preferable, but more expensive. There is an admirable work by Mr. Gough, Principal of the Muir College, Alahabad, on *The Philosophy of the Upanishads and Ancient Indian Meaphysics*. The *Sarva Darsana Sangraha*, translated by Messrs. Gough and Cowell, gives an account of the six schools of philosophy. The *Bhagavad Gita* and *Vedanta Sara* are two other important works under this head.

Further details about books, with the Isa Upanishad quoted in full, and a variety of information, will be found in PHILOSOPHIC HINDUISM, Price 2½ As. sold by Mr. A. T. Scott, Tract Depôt, Madras.

But as already recommended, a beginning should be made with the Rig-Veda. A famous European Philosopher, when dying, is said to have exclaimed, "There is only one man that understands my sytem; and *even he* does not understand it!" Some points in Hindu philosophy are very much disputed.

General Reading.

Christianity, as the religion professed by the most enlightened nations of the world, Social Reform, History, Biography, &c., are other subjects claiming attention. The titles of cheap Publications on them prepared specially for Indian Readers, are given in the following Catalogue, to which attention is invited.

Papers on Religious Reform.

Short Papers for Seekers after Truth. 12mo. 112 pp. 1 An.

A Guide to Religious Inquirers, treating of the Existence of God, Sin, the Need of a Revelation, the leading Doctrines of Christianity, and the Object of Life.

Popular Hinduism. 96 pp. 2½ As. Post-free, 3½ As.

Review of the Hinduism of the Epic Poems and Puranas, &c.; Rites and Observances; Effects of Hinduism, and Suggested Reforms.

Philosophic Hinduism. 72 pp. 2½ As. Post-free, 3 As.

The Upanishads; the Six Schools of Hindu Philosophy; the Minor Schools; Doctrines of Philosophic Hinduism; the Bhagavad Gita; Causes of the Failure of Hindu Philosophy; &c.

An Account of the Vedas, with Illustrative Extracts. 8vo. 166 pp. 4½ As. Post-free, 6 As.

The principal divisions of Vedas are described; with life in Vedic times, the gods of the Vedas, the offerings and sacrifices. Some of the most important hymns from the ten Mandalas are quoted in full. Extracts are also given from the Atharva Veda and the Brahmanas.

The Brahma Samaj, and other Modern Eclectic Religious Systems. 108 pp. 3 As. Post-free, 4 As.

Modern Hindu Theism; Rammohun Roy; Debendranath Tagore; Keshub Chunder Sen; the Sadharan Brahmo Samaj; Madras Brahmoism; Prarthana Samajes; Brahmist Doctrines and Prospects. With Portraits of Rammohun Roy, Debendranath Tagore, and Keshub Chunder Sen.

India Hindu, and India Christian; or, What Hinduism has done for India, and what Christianity would do for it. 8vo. 71 pp. 2½ As. Post-free, 3 As.

Addressed to thoughtful Hindus, showing how much their country would benefit from the religion which many of them now oppose.

Christianity Explained to a Hindu; or, The Doctrines of Christianity and Hinduism Compared. 60 pp. 2 As.

Doctrines about God, Creation, the Soul, Karma, Transmigration, Sin, Incarnations, Salvation, Prospects at Death, and Comparative Effects.

Testimonies of Great Men to the Bible and Christianity. 8vo. 45 pp. 1½ As. Post-free, 2 As.

Opinions expressed by great writers, philosophers, scientists, lawyers, and statesmen, showing that the Bible and Christianity are firmly believed by the most eminent men of the time.

How the People of Ancient Europe became Christians, and the Future Religion of India. 8vo. 48 pp 1½ As. Post-free, 2 As.

An account of the Eastern and Western Aryans; their common origin, resemblances in language and religion; how Christianity was first brought to Europe; the opposition it encountered, and its final success; with the evidence that it will follow a similar course in India.

CIVILIZATION, ANCIENT AND MODERN, COMPARED; WITH REMARKS ON THE STUDY OF SANSKRIT. 8vo. 48 pp. 1½ As. Post-free, 2 As.

Hindu civilization in the Vedic and Puranic Periods, contrasted with that of modern times. The accounts of the former have been largely taken from Mr. R. C. Dutt's *Civilization in Ancient India*. Long extracts are given from Macaulay's celebrated Minute on Indian Education, showing the greater benefits to be derived from Western knowledge than from the study of Sanskrit and Arabic.

LETTERS TO INDIAN YOUTH ON THE EVIDENCES OF CHRISTIANITY. 12mo. 207 pp. 6 Annas. *Eleventh Edition, Revised and Enlarged.*

By the Rev. Dr. Murray Mitchell. External and Internal Evidences of Christianity; Examination of Popular Hinduism, Vedantism, and Muhammadanism.

ELEMENTS OF CHRISTIAN TRUTH. 12mo. 71 pp. 1½ Annas.

Lectures, By the Rev. Dr. Murray Mitchell, delivered to Educated Hindus.

BUSHNELL'S CHARACTER OF JESUS. 18mo. 92 pp. 1½ Annas.
With notes by the Rev. T. E. Slater.

THE CHRISTIAN RELIGION. 12mo. 68 pp.

By Professor Fisher of Yale College, United States, contains replies to some of the objections brought against Christianity.

Papers for Thoughtful Hindus.

No. 1. THE RELATION OF CHRISTIANITY AND HINDUISM. 8vo. 32 pp. By the Rev. Dr. KRISHNA MOHUN BANERJEA, late Sanskrit Examiner to the Calcutta University. ½ Anna.

The remarkable resemblances, in some respects, between ancient Hinduism and Christianity are pointed out.

No. 2. THE SUPPOSED AND REAL DOCTRINES OF HINDUISM, AS HELD BY EDUCATED HINDUS. 8vo. 32 pp. By the Rev. Nehemiah (Nilakanth) Goreh. ½ Anna.

It is shown that the belief of Educated Hindus with regard to God, His Attributes, Creation, &c., are not found in the Vedas, but have been derived from Christianity.

No. 3. MORAL COURAGE. 8vo. 32 pp. ½ Anna.
A lecture by the Bishop of Bombay.

No. 4. THE IMPORTANCE OF RELIGION. 8vo. 48 pp. ¾ Anna.
An appeal to the young, by John Foster, author of Essay on *Decision of Character.*

No. 5. CHRISTIANITY OR—WHAT? 8vo. 16 pp. ¼ Anna.
By Rev. H. Rice. The beneficial results of Christianity are pointed out, and it is shown that no other religion can take its place.

Cheap Reprints of " Present Day Tracts." ½ Anna each.

THE HINDU RELIGION : A SKETCH AND A CONTRAST. 8vo. 43 pp.
By the Rev. Dr. Murray Mitchell. Author of *Letters to Indian Youth on the Evidences of Christianity.*

THE RISE AND DECLINE OF ISLAM. 8vo. 43 pp.
By Sir William Muir, late Lieut.-Governor, North-West Provinces, and Author of a *Life of Mahomet.* With pictures of the Kaaba, Mecca, and Medina.

THE EXISTENCE AND CHARACTER OF GOD. 8vo. 35 pp.
By the Rev. Prebendary Row, M.A.

THE ADAPTATION OF BIBLE RELIGION TO THE NEEDS AND NATURE OF MAN. 8vo. 33 pp.
By the Rev. Dr. Blaikie.

THE WITNESS OF MAN'S MORAL NATURE TO CHRISTIANITY. 8vo. 36 pp.
By the Rev. J. Radford Thomson.

THE CHRIST OF THE GOSPELS : A RELIGIOUS STUDY. 8vo. 27 pp.
By Rev. Henri Mayer, D.D.

The above complete in one volume, half cloth. 6 Annas net.

PAPERS ON SOCIAL REFORM.

ON DECISION OF CHARACTER AND MORAL COURAGE. 8vo. 56 pp. 1½ As. Post-free, 2 As.
A reprint of Foster's celebrated Essay, with some remarks on its application to India.

SANITARY REFORM IN INDIA. 55 pp. 2 As. Post-free, 2½ As.
How lakhs of Lives may be saved every year, and crores of cases of Sickness prevented : Precautions against Fever, Cholera, Diabetes, &c.

Is India becoming Poorer or Richer? With Remedies for the Existing Poverty. 8vo. 82 pp. 2½ As. Post-free, 3 As.
 The prevailing idea with regard to the increasing poverty of India shown to be incorrect, and the true means of promoting its wealth explained.

Debt and the Right Use of Money. 8vo. 32 pp. 1 An.
 Prevalence of Debt in India: its Causes; Evils; how to get out of it; with Franklin's Way to Wealth, &c.

Purity Reform. 8vo. 32 pp. 1 Anna.
 The great need of this reform shown, and the means for its promotion.

Caste. 8vo. 66 pp. 2 As. Post-free, 2¼ As.
 Supposed and real origin of Caste; Laws of Caste according to Manu; its Effects; duty with regard to it.

The Women of India and What can be Done for Them. 8vo. 4 As. Post-free, 5½ As.
 Women in Hindu literature; Female Education; Marriage Customs; Widow Marriage; means to be adopted to raise the position of Women.

The above complete in One volume, 1 Rupee Net. Postage, 2½ As.

Pice Papers on Indian Reform. ¼ Anna Each.

Some are original; others are abridged from the foregoing for popular use.

1. Love of Hoarding and Jewelry.
2. Marriage and Shraddha Expenses.
3. Supposed and Real Causes of Disease.
4. Patriotism: False and True.
5. Management of Infants.
6. Debt, and How to get out of it.
7. The Purdah; or, the Seclusion of Indian Women.
8. Caste: its Origin and Effects.
9. Astrology.
10. What has the British Government done for India?
11. Who wrote the Vedas?
12. Manava-Dharma Sastra.
13. The Bhagavad Gita.
14. The Science of the Hindu Sastras.
15. Fevers: their Causes, Treatment, and Prevention.
16. Cholera and Bowel Complaints.
17. Animal Worship.

18. EARLY MARRIAGE; ITS EVILS, AND SUGGESTED REFORMS.
19. DUTY TO A WIFE.
20. THE FRUITS OF HINDUISM.

THE ABOVE COMPLETE IN ONE VOLUME, 10 Annas.

21. INDIAN WIDOWS AND WHAT SHOULD BE DONE FOR THEM.
22. THE ADVANTAGES OF FEMALE EDUCATION.
23. HINDU AND CHRISTIAN WORSHIP COMPARED.
24. HINDU PILGRIMAGES.
25. CHARITY: FALSE AND TRUE.
26. THE TWO WATCHWORDS—CUSTOM AND PROGRESS.
27. THE VALUE OF PURE WATER.
28. CHARMS, MANTRAS, AND OTHER SUPERSTITIONS.
29. NAUTCHES.
30. THE IMPORTANCE OF CLEANLINESS.
31. HOW TO HAVE HEALTHY CHILDREN.
32. HOW TO BRING UP CHILDREN.

Series for Parents.

CHILDBIRTH. 12mo. 36 pp. 1 Anna. Post-free, 1½ As.
How to have safe delivery, and strong, healthy children.

THE HEALTH OF CHILDREN. 12mo. 106 pp. 2 As.
Management of Infancy; Health; the Diseases of Children, Accidents, short notices of the most useful Medicines.

THE TRAINING OF CHILDREN. 12mo. 94 pp. 2 As. Post-free, 2½ As.
How to train children to be intelligent, obedient, truthful, industrious, orderly &c., showing how to prepare them both for this world and the next.

Descriptions of Countries.

PICTORIAL TOUR ROUND INDIA. Imperial 8vo. 66 pp. 6 As. Post-free, 7½ As.
An imaginary tour round India, with visits to Nepal and Cashmere, describing the principal cities and other objects of interest. With 97 woodcuts illustrative of the Himalayas, Calcutta, Benares, Agra, Delhi, Bombay, Madras, &c.

THE PRINCIPAL NATIONS OF INDIA. 8vo. 160 pp. 4 As. Post-free, 5 As. Full cloth, with gilt title, 10 As.
An account of 42 Nations and Tribes of India, with specimens of some of their languages, and 55 Illustrations.

THE NATIVE STATES OF INDIA AND THEIR PRINCES; WITH NOTICES OF SOME IMPORTANT ZEMINDARIS. 4to. 100 pp. 5 As. Post-free, 6 As.

157 States are described, and 32 portraits are given. The little book will help to enable Indians to understand the vast extent of their country, and what is being done for its improvement.

BURMA AND THE BURMESE. 4to. 54 pp. 2½ As. Post-free, 3 As.

A description of the manners and customs of the Burmese; an account of their government, religion, and history, with illustrative woodcuts, and portraits of King Theebaw and his Queen.

LANKA AND ITS PEOPLE; or, A DESCRIPTION OF CEYLON. 4to. 72 pp. 3 As. Post-free, 3½ As.

The account of Lanka given in the Ramayana is first mentioned. Its history, and present condition are then described, with numerous illustrative woodcuts.

PICTORIAL TOUR ROUND ENGLAND. Royal Quarto. 56 pp. 6 As. Post-free, 7½ As.

Description of the chief places of interest; Public Schools and Universities; English Agriculture and Manufactures; the British Government; Home Life; England an example and warning to India. With 104 woodcuts, and coloured engraving of the Queen-Empress.

PICTURES OF CHINA AND ITS PEOPLE. 4to. 56 pp. 2½ As. Post-free, 3 As.

Extent, History, Manners and Customs of the People; Schools, Examinations; Industries; Travelling; Language and Literature; Government; Religions; India and China compared; with 64 Illustrations.

JAPAN: THE LAND OF THE RISING SUN. 4to. 68 pp. 2½ As. Post-free, 3 As.

With 49 illustrations. An interesting description of this beautiful country, and an account of the remarkable changes which have taken place in it.

ARABIA AND ITS PROPHET. 4to. 64 pp. 2½ As. Post-free, 3 As.

An account of the Arabs, with descriptions of Jeddah, Mecca, Medina; the History of Muhammad, and the early Khalifs; the Koran, Muslim Doctrines, Sects, Prayers, Pilgrimages, &c., with numerous illustrations.

PICTURES OF RUSSIA AND ITS PEOPLES. Imperial 8vo. 83 pp. 5 As. Post-free, 6 As.

A description both of European and Asiatic Russia, including an account of the different races by which they are peopled, their manners and customs, the Government, &c.; with 89 maps and illustrations.

Biographies.

BABA PADMANJI. An Autobiography. 8vo. 108 pp. 2½ As. Post-free, 3 As.

An interesting account by himself of this popular Marathi author, describing his conversion from Hinduism to Christianity.

PICTURE STORIES OF NOBLE WOMEN. 4to. 50 pp. 2½ As. Post-free, 3 As.

Accounts of Cornelia, Agrippina, Padmani of Chittore, Lady Jane Grey, Ahaliya Bai, Mrs. Fry, Princess Alice, Miss Carpenter, Maharani Surnomayi, Pandita Ramabai, Miss Nightingale, and Lady Dufferin.

THE QUEEN-EMPRESS OF INDIA AND HER FAMILY. 43 pp. 3 As. Post-free, 3½ As.

Her early life; marriage; widowhood; children; progress in India during her reign; traits of character and lessons from her life. With 27 illustrations and a coloured portrait of the Empress.

ANGLO-INDIAN WORTHIES: By Henry Morris, Madras C. S., Retired. 8vo. 160 pp. 4 As. Full cloth, gilt title, 10 As.

Lives of Sir Thomas Munro, Sir John Malcolm, Lord Metcalfe, Mountstuart Elphinstone, James Thomason, Sir Henry Lawrence, Sir James Outram, Sir Donald Macleod, and Sir Bartle Frere, with portraits.

EMINENT FRIENDS OF MAN; or, LIVES OF DISTINGUISHED PHILANTHROPISTS. 8vo. 158 pp. 4 As. Post-free, 5 As. Full cloth, gilt title, 10 As.

Sketches of Howard, Oberlin, Granville Sharp, Clarkson, Wilberforce, Buxton, Pounds, Davies of Devauden, George Moore, Montefiore, Livesey, the Earl of Shaftesbury, and others; with remarks on what might be done in India.

SOME NOTED INDIANS OF MODERN TIMES. 8vo. 164 pp. 4 As. Post-free, 5 As.

Sketches of Indian Religious and Social Reformers, Philanthropists, Scholars, Statesmen, Judges, Journalists, and others, with several portraits.

MARTIN LUTHER, THE GREAT EUROPEAN REFORMER. 8vo. 109 pp. 2½ As. Post-free, 3 As.

The state of religion in Europe in the time of Luther is described; a full account is given of his undaunted efforts to bring about a reformation; the greater need of a similar change in India is shown, and Luther is held up as an example. With 15 Illustrations.

(*See also the Anna Library.*)

The Anna Library. 1 Anna, each.

Mostly with Numerous Illustrations.

INDIAN FABLES. 48 pp.
PICTURE FABLES. 48 pp.
CHOICE PICTURES AND STORIES. 48 pp.
PICTURES AND STORIES FOR THE YOUNG. 48 pp.
INDIA IN VEDIC TIMES.
PICTURE STORIES OF THE ANCIENT GREEKS. 48 pp.
PICTURE STORIES OF THE OLD ROMANS. 48 pp.
PICTURE STORIES FROM ENGLISH HISTORY. 48 pp.
PICTURES AND STORIES OF WILD BEASTS. 48 pp.
PICTURE AND STORIES OF BIRDS. 48 pp.
SNAKES, CROCODILES, AND OTHER REPTILES. 48 pp.
CURIOUS LITTLE PEOPLE; A DESCRIPTION OF INSECTS. 48 pp.
THE WONDERFUL HOUSE I LIVE IN. 48 pp.
   A description of the human body.
ASTRONOMY AND ASTROLOGY. 48 pp.
BURNING MOUNTAINS, EARTHQUAKES, AND OTHER WONDERS.
BUDDHA AND HIS RELIGION. 64 pp.
IDOLS OF THE EARTH. 48 pp.
HISTORY OF THE TRUE INCARNATION. 52 pp.
PROVERBS FROM EAST AND WEST. 48 pp.
PALISSY THE POTTER. 48 pp.
WILLIAM CAREY. 48 pp.
   The translator of the Bible into Sanskrit, and the founder of English Missions to India.
STORY OF DR. DUFF, BY A. L. O. E. 56 pp.
GENERAL GARFIELD. 48 pp.
   The farmer boy who became President of the United States.
NEESIMA: THE TRUE PATRIOT OF JAPAN. 48 pp.
   An interesting account of a Japanese who became a sailor to acquire a knowledge of Western learning, and who afterwards founded a Christian University in Japan.
SAINT AUGUSTINE, THE GREATEST EARLY CHRISTIAN WRITER. 48 pp.
DR. LIVINGSTONE, THE GREAT MISSIONARY TRAVELLER. 8vo. 48 pp.

SHORT PAPERS FOR YOUNG MEN. 12mo. 104 pp.
Hints on General Conduct, the Choice of a Profession, and Success in Life.

Miscellaneous.

PICTURES OF WOMEN IN MANY LANDS. Imperial 8vo. 112 pp. 6 As. Post-free, 7½ As.
Descriptions of women, beginning with the most degraded nations of the world, and gradually ascending to the most enlightened; with suggestions, from the review, for Indian women, 172 illustrations.

PICTURES AND STORIES FROM MANY LANDS. 8vo. 97 pp. 2 As. Post-free, 2½ As.
Interesting stories from Asia, Africa, and America, and the islands of the Sea, with 64 illustrations.

PHULMANI AND KARUNA. 8vo. 100 pp. 2 Annas. Post-free, 2½ As.
An interesting tale of Bengali life, by Mrs. Mullens.

PICTURES OF ENGLISH HOME LIFE. 8vo. 80 pp. 2 As.
The object is to give some idea of an English Home. It treats of Houses, Furniture, Servants, Cooking, Food, Amusements, and Training of Children, &c., with 76 illustrations. Educated Hindus might explain it to their wives.

EMBLEMS AND STORIES FOR WOMEN. 8vo. 90 pp. 2 As.
Familiar illustrations of Christian truth taken from domestic life.

THE TWO PILGRIMS TO KASHI AND OTHER STORIES, BY A. L. O. E. 96 pp. 2 As.

JAI SINGH, THE BRAVE SIKH, AND OTHER STORIES, BY A. L. O. E. 92 pp.

THE WONDERFUL MEDICINE AND OTHER STORIES, BY A. L. O. E. 8vo. 2 As.

PICTURE STORIES OF GREAT MEN. 4to. 48 pp. 2 As.
The Lives of Columbus, Peter the Great, Benjamin Franklin, and James Watt.

STORY OF THE FIRST CHRISTIAN MISSIONARY TO EUROPE. 66 pp. 1½ As.
Religious Condition of Ancient Europe; Life of the Apostle Paul.

ILLUSTRATED STORIES FROM HISTORY. 4to. 40 pp. 1½ As.
Interesting stories from the history of different countries, with a number of pictures.

ENGLISH PUBLICATIONS.

STORIES FROM EARLY BRITISH HISTORY. 4to. 40 pp. 1½ As.
An account of the progress of Civilization in early Britain, and how the people became Christians.

STORIES FROM EARLY CHRISTIAN HISTORY. 4to. 28 pp. 1½ As.
State of the world at the beginning of the Christian era; how the Gospel was first brought to Europe; persecutions of the Roman Emperors; accounts of Martyrs; Constantine the first Christian Emperor; with several illustrations.

TRAVELLING BY LAND, ON SEA, AND THROUGH THE AIR. 4to. 18 pp. 1½ As.
Various modes of travelling in different parts of the world, with numerous illustrative woodcuts.

Publications for Indian Students and Teachers.

SELECT CONVOCATION ADDRESSES, delivered to Graduates of the Madras University. 8vo. 231 pp. Stiff covers, 8 As.; Half bound in cloth, 12 As. Full bound in cloth, with gilt title, 1 Re. Post-free.
The volume contains 15 addresses, commencing in 1859, and including the most recent. Some of the most distinguished men in South India during the last 30 years took part in the Series. Many very useful hints to young men entering upon the battle of life in any part of India will be found in the collection.

THE INDIAN STUDENT'S MANUAL. 12mo. 352 pp. 8 As. Post-free, 9 As.
Hints on Studies, Examinations, Moral Conduct, Religious Duties, and Success in Life.

THE RESPONSIBILITIES OF STUDENTS. 8vo. 32 pp. ½ Anna.
A Lecture by N. G. Chandavarker, Esq., B.A., B.L.

HOW TO PASS EXAMINATIONS. 8vo. 29 pp. ½ Anna.
Advice to students about University Examinations, with an account of a great examination which all must pass.

PRAYERS FOR STUDENTS AND OTHERS. 18 mo. 36 pp. ½ Anna.

THE SCHOOL-BOY. 16mo. 48 pp. ¾ Anna.
Advice to school-boys about their lessons, general conduct, and duty to God.

Orders to be addressed to Mr. A. T. SCOTT, Tract Depôt, Memorial Hall Compound, MADRAS; or to the Depôts mentioned on the last page of the Wrapper.

www.ingramcontent.com/pod-product-compliance
Lightning Source LLC
Chambersburg PA
CBHW021918180426
43199CB00032B/705